THE TURKEY FARM
BEHIND THE SMILE

Cheryl Archer and Jennifer Keefe

THE TURKEY FARM - BEHIND THE SMILE DISCLAIMER:

Based on a true story, this is Jennifer's perception, opinion and recollection of the events that shaped her life. Some names, dates and places in this book have been changed for privacy and protection.

Copyright 2005 Cheryl Archer and Jennifer Keefe
All rights reserved. No part of this publication may be reproduced, stored in a retrieval system, or transmitted, in any form or by any means, electronic, mechanical, photocopying, recording, or otherwise, without the written prior permission of the authors.

Note for Librarians: A cataloguing record for this book is available from the ISBN Registration Agency or at www.isbn.org

Dedication

This book is dedicated to our children, Katelyn, Ian, Ryan, Stephanie, Jaran and Sam, who have been our biggest fans through this journey. You have always believed in our dream and sacrificed precious time with your moms to make it come true. This dedication is only one way of showing ALL of you how truly proud we are that you call us mom.

Tribute

I started this book as a means for me to express my feelings in an effort to bring understanding and healing within myself. But as I came to the end I realized that it was also a way for me to get to know my parents who were taken from me very early in life, one by force the other by choice. More importantly, it is a tribute to my mother, Patricia. In my heart of hearts I know she has always been with me. I have felt her presence and can think of no other reason how I could have made it through the perils of life without her spiritual guidance.

As time passed after her death she faded into my subconscious. She became an image I had created in my mind rather then a person I had once known and loved. Eventually I felt I didn't know her at all and even began to question the choices she had made. In finding my own truths I discovered a woman I am proud to call my mom.

Patricia (Patty) Keefe

Acknowledgements

    There are many people we would like to thank for helping to make this book possible - the believers who never lost hope in us and even the non-believers who made us never lose hope. The journey was long, but there are some much deserving family and friends that we want to send a shout-out to for their help in bringing this dream to fruition:

    Mike Archer, for sacrificing time with your wife so she could spend endless hours writing; Mike Kleinpeter, Roger Kleinpeter, Barry Eastman, Kim Plancon, Ben Sanders, Steven Murdock, Linda "Nard" Turner for investing in our dream and helping to make it possible; The women at the Grafton County Court House, and, the Federal Bureau in Concord, New Hampshire and the Federal Bureau in Washington, DC, for retrieving files from the archives; the Concord State Prison for your compassion; Roland Bixby and Cory Blake for teaching us the business aspect of the literary world; and our fabulous editor Ellen Beck.

Prologue

On February 26, 1981 darkness besieged me and held tightly for over twenty-five years. My adulthood had become one big identity crisis with no sense of belonging or purpose. As a child, I had often wondered if there really was a God and why he was punishing me. What had I done to deserve so many terrible things at such a young age?

As I traveled back in time to the place where it had all been taken away from me – the place my mother believed would be better but which proved to be the most damaging for me – I began the journey of taking back my life.

"Fate has not been kind to you," my best friend Cheryl whom I've always called Sha said as we drove up the familiar road. "By all rights, Jen, you should be really messed up."

"Yeah, sometimes I feel my life is like a bad movie," I replied ruefully. "Looking back from an adult perspective, I am horrified by what I remember. When I compare the way I was raised to how I'm raising my own children, it kills me to recall the things I was exposed to at their age." I pointed to the stream that ran beside the road. "That brook represents so much. I remember the baths James and I took in it, and lugging the heavy buckets of water to the little shack we lived in before the main house was built. We had secret hiding places amongst the rocks and fallen trees."

There were other milestones along the road, and as I remembered them I would share each story.

"James and I had to walk this windy dirt road every day—rain, sleet or snow—to catch the bus. It was a good two miles."

"And my kids complain about a measly hundred feet!" Sha responded with a laugh.

An eerie feeling came over me as the turkey farm came into view. It had been years since I'd been there and I had to catch my breath. The once beautiful and thriving farm was now rundown and desolate. As soon as we pulled up in front of the house, a kaleidoscope of memories flooded my mind. A light shone in the front window and a lone car was parked in the driveway.

"Someone must live here," I said. "I never did find out what happened to the farm after the federal government seized it and we were forced to move."

After sitting in the car for a few minutes, I mustered up the courage to approach the house. As I walked up the familiar steps and knocked on the wooden door, I was overwhelmed by the vision of it being busted open. Instantly, I was a seventeen-year-old junior in high school again.

"May I help you?" a plump woman asked as she opened the heavy door, cautiously peeking around it. A middle-aged, frumpy woman with a plain grey skirt and brown department store shoes, she reminded me of the children's storybook character "Old Mother Hubbard."

"Hello, my name is Jennifer and I grew up here," I said nervously, unsure how the woman would react. "I was wondering if I could look around a little."

The woman's face brightened. She opened the door wider and motioned for us to come in. "I've heard a lot of stories about this place," she said matter-of-factly and then proceeded to tell us everything she knew about the farm and the people associated with it. "I heard the young mother who lived here was murdered and that her head was cut off. And that the police found human bones in the well out back."

Even after learning that I was the child of the woman who had died in the house, she never stopped talking about all the rumors she'd heard and assumed were true. I was shocked by her lack of consideration for my feelings as she babbled on about what she believed had happened at the infamous turkey farm.

Ignoring her version of what reportedly occurred the night my mother died, I allowed myself to go back in time. As I stood in the living room, my childhood flashed before me. Everything looked the same except the living room furniture, which had been replaced with office equipment. Evidently, the farm had been turned into some sort of security business.

"I guess the man who killed her also raped her," the woman continued, "and her husband was off on a drug deal when it happened. Most of the townspeople believe he was behind her death and that it was a result of his drug dealings."

A knot in my stomach started to develop as I listened to the insensitive woman go on and on about all the untruths she believed to be fact. I knew rumors had flown for years after my mom's death, but I hadn't realized they were so vicious. When she mentioned that my mother had been raped, I could feel my blood begin to boil. That was one piece of information I hadn't verified, and to hear her say it made me feel violated—not for myself but for my mom. I tried very hard to keep my composure and not allow her ignorance to get to me. Acting as if nothing she was saying fazed me, I allowed a big smile to cross my face and walked over to the staircase.

"Bill had a professional wood-burner come in to do these pictures of wildlife on the base of the staircase," I said, running my hand along the railing. "Originally there was a spiral staircase here, but after my mother died Bill had it removed. Strangely, he kept it behind a locked door in the barn." *I wonder why*, I thought to myself, but said, "I wonder if it's still there."

"The man who owns the property now has been searching for the secret underground tunnel the newspapers reported," the woman piped up, "but he hasn't been able to find it. You must know where it's located," she asked, clearly hoping I would lead her to it. "I also heard there's a BMW filled with money buried out back."

"You really shouldn't believe everything you hear, ma'am," I responded with a chuckle. "And I can assure you that, contrary to popular belief, if there is a car buried out back, there's nothing in it now."

By that point, I had had enough of her rudeness and decided that if she wanted information I would give her information. I knew that once Sha and I had departed, this woman would be left all alone with the visuals I was about to give her.

"The truth of it is that this woodstove right here is where my mother fought courageously for her life while she was being beaten with a fire-poker. And the bathroom over there is where my two-year-old brother was locked away in the cold darkness until someone rescued him two days later. Those stairs that lead to the basement are where my mother's lifeless body was found."

That'll teach her, I thought as the woman sat speechless behind her desk. When her telephone rang, she made no move to answer it. Her disposition had noticeably changed and she now appeared eager to hear the truth. So I left her with one last tidbit.

"After my mom died strange things used to happen around here and her presence could always be felt. She was a very spiritual person, and I have no doubt that she was and still is watching over my brothers and me."

Just then, a heavy object in the upstairs bedroom fell to the floor. Startled, all three of us jumped.

"Well, I've taken up enough of your time," I said, satisfied the woman was sufficiently freaked out. "Thank you for letting me come back and reminisce."

When we left the farm that day, I could almost hear the telephone wires burning. I was sure the old lady was calling everyone she knew and telling them she had just spoken to the daughter of the murdered woman from Bill's Turkey Farm.

    Although I can visit the cemetery any time, the farm is where I feel my mom is. Being there that day made me feel even closer to her. I had never realized how far away from her I felt until being there that day. It made me want more than ever to talk with her and ask her all the things a child wants to know about her parents. Since that was impossible, I decided to go to the next best thing—her best friend Nard. I hadn't seen or spoken to Nard in years, but the moment I heard her voice I became a young child again. As soon as she began to recount the tales of her youth with my parents, I could tell that she, too, was slipping back in time.

    I was grateful for the glimpse into my mother's past. My previous memories of her had been from a child's viewpoint. I couldn't help but wonder how someone who had grown up in a typical All-American family could have fallen into a lifestyle that was so drastically different. After learning about her environment and how the changes happening in the world at that time deeply influenced the choices my mother made – choices that would severely impact not only her life but mine as well – I felt like I was beginning to reconnect with her as an adult.

Chapter One

    Men wanted her and women wanted to be like her. My mom, Patricia (Patty) Keefe, was a beautiful, petite woman (about five foot three and 110 pounds) with long, blond hair and hazel eyes. She was an alluring, free spirited, everything-in-moderation girl with a knack for captivating everyone with whom she came in contact. Everyone who engaged in a conversation with her knew they had her undivided attention. The expression on her face and the way she smiled was as inviting as it was accepting. Unfortunately, it was her genuine compassion for people and her willingness to help them that may have cost my mother her life.

    The middle child of a prominent Catholic family, Patty was born in October 1949. Raised in Wakefield, an affluent suburb of Boston, Massachusetts, she grew up in an era when families spent time together, family values were everything and belief in God was never questioned. She went to church faithfully, attended Sunday school and made her first holy communion. A strong family foundation with morals and integrity was the basis of my mother's upbringing. Divorce was rare in those days, and with the security of a two-parent home, kids were allowed to be kids. People believed that children who had a happy childhood would become responsible productive adults. Parents had plenty of time to spend with each other and their children. A man's role was clear-cut: to make the money necessary to provide for his family. And there was no greater job for a woman than to be a wife and mother. Women took pride in providing emotional support to their children, teaching proper etiquette and instilling in them values, morals and integrity. The media didn't tolerate anything that had an unhealthy impact on children, so TV shows and movies always had a positive message and heroes who "did the right thing."

In the 1950s, families had a strong sense of "God and Country." The golden rule "Do unto others as you would have them do unto you" was the key moral that adults practiced and taught to their children. Religion had a strong influence on everyday life, and children knew about the Bible and its importance. Patriotism was just as important as religion, especially after the United States helped to end the aggression of the Nazis and Japanese in World War II. It was also a stricter, more structured time. Authority was respected and appreciated because people believed in the greater good of society. Rules were important and not often broken. When they were, people were held accountable for their wrongdoing. People paid for the consequences of their actions.

But by the end of the 1950s, in-your-face rebellion had begun to surface. The saying, "Children are to be seen and not heard" was tested to the very limit. In 1956, Elvis Presley emerged with a new genre, rock 'n' roll, exploding on the entertainment scene and causing controversy on the Ed Sullivan Show. His pelvic thrusting and leg-shaking had teenage fans delirious with adoration. He represented a more carefree attitude, and young America was hungry for it. Parents feared that by watching him their children would turn into juvenile delinquents.

By the early 1960s, over seventy million post-war baby boomers had become teenagers, and my mother was one of them. "Experimentation" was the catch word of this era. The movement from the conservative '50s had resulted in a revolutionary mode of thought that became selfish and carefree. The traditional rules about sex, relationships, politics and drugs were thrown out the window as this rebellious generation questioned everything. They wanted change and they got it, fumbling their way through a sea of obscure morals, values and beliefs. Long-standing attitudes about education, government, lifestyle, laws, music and movies were challenged.

This new way of thinking brought extreme changes to the cultural fabric of American life and the youth became vulnerable to what was happening around them. Poodle skirts were replaced by mini-skirts and go-go boots. Girls went from bouffant hairdos to allowing their long locks to hang down their backs. Guys grew out their traditional crew-cuts and sported long hair as well. Tie-dyed bandanas and acid-colored clothing with love beads were "right on" for teenagers across the country. Parents could no longer shield their children from the ways of the world as television increasingly influenced them by programming what was going on across the nation, bringing social experiments into living rooms everywhere.

In early 1960 a new and young president named John F. Kennedy was elected into office. He symbolized motivation and inspiration and dreams for a new generation with statements like "...Let the word go forth from this time and place to friend and foe alike, that the torch has passed to a new generation of Americans born in this century, tempered by war, disciplined by a hard and bitter peace, proud of our ancient heritage" and "...Ask not what your country can do for you but what you can do for your country."

My mother was fourteen years old and in junior high when President John F. Kennedy was assassinated in his motorcade in Dallas, Texas in 1963. At around the same time, she met Jimmy Keefe, a funny, kind-hearted boy. Although he came from a family unlike hers, they felt they were soul mates, and a large group of friends viewed them as the perfect couple.

Throughout the rest of the '60's, the only thing the country could count on was change. As the United States' role in the Vietnam War dramatically escalated, so did society's reaction. The values young America had been taught as children seemed to unravel. Respect for authority declined and crime soared. The Supreme Court ruled that prayer in schools was unconstitutional and many youth turned from their traditional religious beliefs to mystical eastern religions. The strong women's movement influenced changes in the family unit and divorce became more acceptable.

Harvard professor-turned-drug-guru Timothy Leary advocated the use of hallucinogenic drugs, stating, "An LSD trip is a religious experience that will transform your life." These mind-expanding drugs reached the burgeoning hippie community whose message was peace, love, acceptance and understanding. They figured that if using marijuana encouraged thoughts *about* God, then an LSD trip would be like experiencing the world *as* God. These psychedelic drugs provided insight and encouraged thoughts uninhibited by tradition—modern-day apples from the Garden of Eden.

The '60s produced an incredible musical talent, a direct result of the drugs that opened minds and unleashed a barrage of new ideas on society. At the time, there was widespread uncertainty about the future. Drugs and music helped to ease the pain. The messages in the lyrics reflected what was going on in the world, from the war in Vietnam to protests and demonstrations all across the United Sates. Songs like "Lucy in the Sky with Diamonds" by The Beatles and "Give Peace a Chance" by John Lennon became indicative of the times. Despite the fact that most, if not all, the bands that were popular during this era were on drugs, few would disagree that their messages were profound. Now, almost four decades later, this music is considered classic and continues to serve as a reminder of where our country has been and perhaps where we are going.

As teenagers, Wakefield's Common was the place everyone hung out. It was peaceful, and my mom loved to become "one with nature." Birds chirped high above the trees as squirrels scurried in playful synchrony. Surrounding the small pond called Lake Quannapowitt was a walking path that led to downtown Main Street where the bandstand held concerts in the summer.

A typical afternoon for Patty, Jimmy and their friends would involve hanging out in the Common. Sitting cross-legged in a circle under a huge oak tree that provided just the right amount of shade from the blazing July sun, the gang would groove to the music while Jimmy, in his Salvation Army attire, strummed on his guitar. His brown, shoulder-length hair hung over his face as he swayed back and forth to the rhythm of the song he played. The rest of the group would sing a familiar Bob Dylan tune as they passed around a "joint." Barefoot and wearing a white peasant tank top and long, flowing skirt, Patty would get up and begin to dance, her blond, straw-like hair cascading down her back as she twirled around and around. Soon her two best friends, Nard and Linda, would join in. Coming from similar backgrounds, the three of them had been friends since grade school. In their innocence, they had promised to stay friends forever and became blood-sisters to seal the bond. Proving their devotion, each girl made a cut in the palm of her right hand and then put them together. This symbolic gesture demonstrated their unbreakable bond. The pact would prove true as their friendship prevailed through the darkest of times over the years.

During the summer of 1967, people everywhere flocked to the Haight-Ashbury section of San Francisco. Thousands came together to hear free concerts from an array of new artists such as The Mamas and the Papas, Jefferson Airplane, Grateful Dead and The Doors. Seventeen-year-old Patty and her friends, Nard and Linda, piled in the back of Jimmy's powder-blue Ford Vista and headed west to join in the "Summer of Love." While the rest of the country was being ravaged by the war and the civil rights movement, they figured they would do just as well to heed drug guru Timothy Leary's advice and "tune in, turn on, drop out" with the rest of young America.

Even though they knew no one and had little money and no place to stay, they found a whole city of allies who offered them food, shelter and drugs—a festival of colorful bohemian communities indulging in the ideals of the time: peace, love, harmony, music and mysticism. When they arrived at "hippie haven," the gang found a "pub"—a little hole in the wall that offered them a place to grab a beer and figure out what to do next. Taking a seat at the bar, Patty noticed they were the only ones in the place.

The bartender, a friendly soft-spoken man with long hair pulled back into a ponytail, approached them. "What'll it be, kids?"

"Hey, man, we'll have whatever's on tap," Jimmy said.

"Right on," the bartender said, as he pulled four frosted mugs from the cooler. "Where ya'll from?"

"The east coast," Jimmy replied. "Massachusetts."

"I bet you came to see history in the making," the bartender stated emphatically, as he set their beers down in front of them.

"So where can we find all the excitement?" Patty spoke up. She was eager to see all the sights she had heard about on the news.

"I'm off work in a half-hour. I'll show you around," the bartender offered. "By the way, my name's Michael."

"Out-a-sight. Thanks, man," Jimmy said before introducing himself with a handshake. "This is my old lady Patty and her friends, Nard and Linda."

While walking down Market Street, the main drag, Michael, a transplant from the mid-west and aspiring artist, explained how he had lived in San Francisco for three years. He told them about all the hotspots in the city and how to get there and shared many of his experiences so far. As they walked towards the panhandle and Golden Gate Park, the main site for all the festivities, they popped into a head shop on the corner of Fulton and Masonic Street. These specialty shops offered a wide selection of paraphernalia for the new age—herbal smokes and accessories, incense and oils, candles and tapestries.

"So Michael my man, you must know where we can score," Jimmy said.

"What'll it be, my friend," Michael asked, pulling a baggie out of his front pocket. "You interested in a blotter?"

"LSD?" Patty inquired with interest.

"One drop will take you on a trip of a lifetime pretty lady," Michael said as he handed each of them a tiny blue square.

Realizing that none of them had ever experienced the ride of acid, he explained that the effects and reaction to the hallucinogenic drug were strongly determined by a person's mindset and surroundings. He advised them to enjoy and embrace where it would take them. "Just let yourself go," he said soothingly.

Twenty minutes after placing the tiny piece of paper on her tongue, Patty felt a sense of euphoria. Her body tingled as she became increasingly aware of the sights and sounds around her. The instruments of a band playing two blocks away were magical; she thought she had never heard anything so beautiful before. As the sun began to set over the Pacific Ocean, the orange, red and yellow colors were so vivid it took Patty's breath away. She knew that she'd never see a sunset like that again, and as it disappeared into the crystal blue water it took away all her inhibitions. She watched it ripple and shimmer until it was gone.

At that very moment, Patty fell in love with herself and life and the people around her. She saw every object, every person, every experience in a whole new light. This heightened insight into herself and the world allowed her to become aware of things that were normally filtered out by the mind. It was a blissful feeling, and Patty wanted it to stay with her forever. The taste of such insight made her want to know more.

The group of friends came upon a storefront with a neon sign in the window that said "Psychic Readings." Having just connected with herself, Patty decided she wanted to have her future told. A rather large woman wearing a long colorful robe and bandana-like turban sat at a small round table. Candles and incense burned throughout the tiny room as the woman meditated before telling Patty to sit down. Extending both arms across the table, she gestured for Patty to do the same. The psychic turned Patty's hands palm side up and began massaging them over and over before tracing her fingers along each line from finger to wrist.

"You've had a wonderful life, my child," she said confidently. "You have many hopes and dreams for the future." A long pause was replaced by a deep and sympathetic sigh as the psychic continued. "But you have a very short lifeline, you see here," she said as she showed Patty the line in the middle of her palm. "My dear, you are going to die a young and tragic death."

"Wow!"

"Sweet child, he will come like a thief in the night," the psychic said with concern.

"Far out!" Patty exclaimed as she got up and walked away. Perhaps it was the acid talking but even though Patty believed the reading to be true, she wasn't frightened. However she would never forget her foretold future.

As the gang continued their guided tour of the hotspots of San Francisco, the euphoria Patty felt was suddenly replaced by a hollow sense of artificial phoniness. Her mind raced in slow motion. *Who am I?* she thought. Realizing that her whole life had been based on everyone else's opinion – parents, teachers, friends, media – Patty began to question everything about herself. Wondering where the insightfulness she'd felt a few hours earlier had gone, Patty stood on the edge of the curb as cars zoomed by. The colors of the vehicles looked as though they were melting into one another. It was as if she could see sound and hear color. Their destination, Golden Gate Park, was in front of her and Patty wondered if this would be her tragic death like the psychic predicted.

Suddenly, Patty felt intensely overwhelmed. Squatting to the ground, she wrapped her arms around herself in a hug. Rocking back and forth, she felt as though she'd stepped outside her body and could see inside her soul. She began contemplating her whole life. Molecule by molecule, she re-assessed her past, present and future. At that moment, she decided to embrace every opportunity and savor every day as if it were her last. Patty took the gold Timex watch her parents had given her as a graduation gift and threw it into the traffic.

"What'd you do that for?" Nard, who had sat down beside her, asked.

"To be free of time," Patty responded with a new sense of being. "I have been reborn," she announced as she jumped up and headed towards the park.

"Groovy," Nard said as she followed her friend.

My mother's week in San Francisco was one she would never forget. She never did LSD again, but the insights and feelings she experienced were life-changing. When she returned to Wakefield, she continued her carefree lifestyle and took some time off before deciding on college and career. She remained close with Nard and Linda, and her relationship with Jimmy grew stronger.

When Linda found out she was pregnant shortly after they returned from the west coast, however, things changed. Reality soon hit, as Patty realized the freedoms they were all experiencing also had consequences. Times may have been different, but it was still unacceptable for an unwed teenager to have a baby. When Linda's parents sent her away to live with family in Florida until her "ordeal" was over, Patty's heart broke for her best friend. Despite Linda's boyfriend professing his love for her, they were forced apart, the "shame" hidden away until it could be given away.

In the fall of 1969, following the infamous Woodstock, Patty learned she, too, was pregnant. Surprised but happy, she and Jimmy did the right thing and married shortly before I was born in May 1970. They named me Jennifer Rae. Four months later, to my mother's shock, she became pregnant again. In June 1971, she gave birth to my brother, James Jr. She was only twenty-one years old. We lived in a rented one-bedroom basement apartment. Mom didn't mind being cramped in such small quarters because it was located in a decent part of Wakefield. James and I shared the bedroom while my parents' bed was the pullout couch in the living room.

Ironically, Nard became pregnant around the same time and had a baby boy. She, too, married her high school sweetheart. With their lives on similar paths, Patty and Nard found themselves leaning on one another for guidance and support. Although they still liked to have a good time once in awhile and occasionally indulged in some extra-curricular activities, partying was no longer their main priority. Building a family had become their focus.

When Linda returned from Florida a year and a half later, she found it difficult to be around her two best friends who had set up the kind of life she had wanted. Both were now married with babies, which increased the emotional stress she was experiencing regarding her own "situation." Saddened by the constant reminder of the child she had given up, Linda abused drugs to ease her pain. Not wanting to turn her back on her friend, my mom tried desperately to help Linda. In an effort to get her away from the self-destructive behavior she was embracing, she introduced Linda to a guy she knew named Tommy. Within six months they were married and pregnant and Linda no longer felt like the odd man out.

All three of them had settled down and life couldn't be better, or so they thought.

Chapter Two

Although the Vietnam War was over, the country continued to be divided. People tried to find meaning in a now spiritually empty society that was in a state of moral decay. Having lost close friends in Vietnam to either death or emotional devastation, my dad, who was easily lured by drugs and alcohol, was drinking heavily. Like his own father, Jimmy was becoming an alcoholic and didn't grasp the importance of working and providing for his family. He was a great guy, would give you the shirt off his back, but he just couldn't hold down a job.

Mom knew that in order to give her children the life she wanted she would have to get a good job, which meant she needed an education. Her dream was to become a pediatric nurse, so she started taking classes while working part-time at a convenience store. However, the strain of her busy life eventually took its toll on my parents and their marriage. Jimmy wasn't showing any signs of growing up. He didn't work, was drinking all the time and unable to care for James and me in my mom's absence. Clearly, starting a family hadn't changed my dad's perspective on what was important in life.

One night after working all day and going to school all night, Mom came home to a screaming baby. James was standing in his crib with a soaking wet diaper, dirty T-shirt and snot running out of his nose from crying for so long. It was obvious he was hungry. When Mom opened the refrigerator to get a bottle, only to discover there wasn't any milk, she realized she couldn't live like that any longer. As usual all she found was a six-pack of Schlitz beer. Looking at my dad who had passed out on the couch, she shook her head in disgust.

Saddened because my dad was the love of her life, and desperately wanting him to step up to the plate, Patty did the unthinkable. She left her husband of three years, not because she didn't love him but because she needed and wanted more than he would give. My mom truly did love my dad with all her heart and knew he loved his family, too. But he loved his drinking more. Hoping a separation would force him to wake up and realize what was important, Mom waited a while before filing for divorce. But my dad never did "wake up" and would spend the rest of his life in regret.

I'll never forget the day my parents' divorce became final. Pushing open the screen door, I ran from the house and sat on the swing that hung from a maple tree in our front yard. I was angry—not at my mom, but at my dad for making my mom so sad. I knew she still loved him, and when I asked her why he didn't love her back, my mom said, "Daddy does love me, Jenny. It's just that his love is upside down."

"Can't you make it stand up again?" I asked innocently, as she pushed me lightly on the swing.

"It's not that simple, honey. Daddy and I know each other too well," Mom said with a sigh.

It took me years to fully understand what she meant by that.

For the first few months after my parents divorce we lived with my mom's folks. Nana and Pa had a finished basement that was turned into a small apartment. My brother and I shared a bed on one side of the room, while a make-shift wall of hanging blankets separated us from Mom's bed on the other side. We had lived there only a few months before Nana caught my mom sneaking a guy in late one night. This incident resulted in a huge fight between Mom and Nana. After that, we stayed with Nard (who was also divorced) for a few nights until Mom was able to get her own place.

Still passionate about obtaining her nursing degree, Mom took an apartment in the low-income housing section of town and went on welfare. It was the only way she could complete school while raising two young children. We lived in the "projects" for the next two years. With no help from my dad, Mom couldn't afford day care and was forced to use teenage babysitters for James and me. One time our babysitters took us to their school, where they broke in and ransacked the classrooms. We crawled in through a ground level window and James and I watched as they knocked over desks and chairs and threw papers all over the floor. Mom's determination to finish school forced her to ignore certain things, including our going on rebellious excursions with delinquent teenagers.

Although my memories of our time living in the "projects" are random there are certain ones that were significant enough to leave a lasting impression on me. One night I was taking a bath while my mom was in the bathroom getting ready to go out with her friends. I decided I wanted to be grown-up and shave my legs like my mommy did. I had seen her shave before and I wanted to try it, too. As she put on her makeup and fixed her hair I grabbed the razor lying on the side of the tub and ran it up the entire length of my shin without soap or anything. Blood started to gush everywhere. Convinced I was going to die, I screamed. Mom turned around with a jerk, startled at my sudden cries. When she saw what I had done she calmly took the razor from my hand and told me I shouldn't touch her things without permission. She cleaned and bandaged my leg, then sealed it with a kiss before going out with her friends. I still have that scar on my shin to this day and whenever I notice it I'm reminded of how lovingly my mom cared for it, and me.

Mom graduated as an LPN (Licensed Practical Nurse) in June of 1975. Even my dad showed up at her graduation. Everyone was proud of her accomplishment, especially Nana and Pa, who weren't particularly pleased that she was a divorced, single parent. They wanted a better life for her. Now with a nursing degree Nana and Pa were hopeful their daughter was headed in the right direction, especially for the sake of my brother and me.

Just as Mom was beginning a new chapter in her life, she met Bill. Actually, Linda was dating Bill at the time, but the minute he met Patty he was immediately smitten by her charming smile and sexy good looks. Her independence intrigued him and her funny, warm personality made him melt. Bill wanted to take care of her and her two children and give her all the things she deserved but never had with Jimmy. An entrepreneur of sorts, Bill was a self-proclaimed driftwood salesman with tons of money and a generosity my mother found exciting—the opposite of what she'd been used to with my dad.

An enigmatic man, Bill Dalton was six feet four with black hair, matching black eyes and olive skin, remnants from his distant Indian ancestry. On his right forearm was a picture of the devil and the words "Born to Raise Hell," which summed him up quite well. He had a powerful physical presence that was very intimidating. Some people disliked Bill initially, others were fearful of him, most women were fascinated. Eager to win James and me over, he would always bring us jelly beans, so we used to call him the "jelly bean man."

Bill was the second of four children, raised in Boston by an overbearing and controlling father. Early on, he realized that making money was easy if you were willing to take risks. He chose a path of destruction, starting in his teens with petty crimes like stealing cars. Then he succumbed to the irresistible lure of drugs. Like most teens, he thought he was invincible. When he was eighteen years old, after a few run-ins with the law, Bill held up a pharmacy. Thinking he could outsmart them, he ran but ended up being cornered by the cops. He was shot in the back during the pursuit. Unable to safely remove the bullet, doctors left it lodged near his spine (where it remains to this day).

Bill was sentenced to five years at Walpole prison for that crime but only served three. During those years he read everything he could get his hands on, most notably *Readers Digest* and *National Geographic*. He has a gift for retaining all he reads, so he became highly informed and knowledgeable in many areas. He was released early for good behavior but was still considered a felon. If he kept his nose clean, he would be afforded the right to clear his name. I wouldn't say Bill ever straightened out; he just got better at not getting caught. Even after the appropriate amount of time had expired, Bill never filed the proper paperwork. His misadventures as a teenager would later send him back to prison as an adult.

Despite his run-ins with the law Patty found Bill exciting. She started to see the possibilities and embrace the notion that she wouldn't have to live in poverty much longer. It wasn't long before she gave up working and moved into a house Bill had bought for her in a quaint neighborhood in an upscale part of Stoneham, Massachusetts. The beige, three-bedroom, split-level house was located on a dead-end street named Webster Court. In the foyer at the front of the house were two sets of red shag carpeted stairs. One set led up to the main part of the house —the living room, dining room, kitchen and a bathroom. The second set of stairs led to a dimly lit downstairs studio apartment with one bedroom, a bathroom and an efficiency kitchen. There was a third floor containing three rarely-used bedrooms. The studio apartment is where Mom and Bill slept and spent most of their time partying with friends late into the night after us kids went to bed. Mom turned the dining room on the main floor into a bedroom for James and me to share – I assume because it was closer to where she was downstairs.

Some of my earliest and fondest memories are from our time on Webster Court. I will never forget our first Christmas there. The year was 1976. Bill and Mom had been up all night partying and wrapping presents. At around 4:00 AM they came running into our room yelling, "Hurry! Santa is here and you're going to miss him!" We came stumbling out, only to find that we had missed Santa. But what we found was amazing. The living room had been filled to the ceiling with more presents than I had ever seen. Right in the middle of it all were two brand new bikes!

When we first moved to Webster Court James and I had only each other to play with (except for Nard and Linda's kids Shawn and Becky whenever they were over). The street was lined with houses, ours being the last one nestled beside a wooded area that led to a quarry. Wooded areas aren't common in Massachusetts, so it was an exciting jungle playground for us. After a while we noticed a group of older kids hanging around the neighborhood. James and I would stand on the sidewalk in front of our house and yell, tease and taunt them as they played ball in the street. When the big kids were out riding their bikes we would follow them from a distance which is how we found the tree fort they'd made in the woods behind our house. Eventually, they gave in and let us tag along with them. These kids were much older than we were—maybe eleven or twelve (at the time, James and I were five and six, respectively), but we wanted to be "cool" like them.

Being the 70's it was the disco era and music from ABBA and Fleetwood Mac played constantly in our house. Fashion had changed yet again. Mom wore hip-huggers, platform shoes and mood rings. Bill sported shoulder-length hair, bell bottom pants and T-shirts featuring his favorite rock band. The house was always filled with their friends. Nard and Linda were over almost every day with their kids, and even lived with us for a short time. Drugs were still generally accepted among society and cocaine was now the addiction of the time. It wasn't unusual for me to walk downstairs to where Mom and Bill slept and find a mirror surrounded by candied fruit, white lines in the middle and a rolled-up hundred dollar bill lying next to it. Bill loved little hard candies and was always popping them, I assume to combat perpetual dry mouth. The money was used as a straw to snort the lines.

Shortly after we moved to Webster Court Mom and Bill became submerged in the crazy life of cocaine addiction. People did drugs freely—even the "big" kids we hung out with. Although they weren't doing cocaine, they were smoking marijuana. One time they left some remnants in the tree fort and my little brother James and I found it. We rolled up a leaf and tried to light it. That's all it was, a rolled-up pot leaf, but we thought we were the coolest thing! Then we found a pack of cigarettes they had hidden in the tree fort. We decided we wanted to try that out too. Bill caught us and he got so mad that he hauled James and me back to the house and made us smoke one cigarette after another until we were sick. I can honestly say that I never smoked cigarettes again...until high school.

Sex was a big part of the culture, too. Monogamy wasn't a word I understood until much later in life. I saw lots of people doing it with lots of people. Sometimes my brother and I would peak through a crack in the bedroom door or window and watch – its how I learned about the birds and the bees.

For a while my mom and Bill would party all night and sleep all day, leaving me to assume the parental responsibilities. (To her credit, Mom always made sure we had clean clothes set out to wear and food to eat.) I must have had a natural maternal instinct because I never minded taking care of James. I enjoyed being the "big helper." It made me feel important and grown-up. For a time, she relied on me to get James up in the morning, dressed, fed and off to school. However, being I was still a kid, on a couple of occasions teachers had to come to the house because we hadn't been to school in a few days, opting instead to stay home and watch "Mighty Mouse" cartoons.

Within a year, and after countless all-nighters, Bill and my mom began having drug-induced physical fights in the middle of the night. For some unknown reason, sometimes they were naked. I would wake up to screaming and yelling and the sound of objects hitting the wall.

As those nights became increasingly frequent and the intensity of their brawls unbearable, I would hide under my blanket and shake from fear. I'd pray to God that it would stop before someone got hurt, or worse, killed. But despite my young age, deep down I knew they were fighting because of the drugs, not because they hated each other.

One night I awakened to my mom screaming and the sound of flesh being smacked. In my favorite Strawberry Shortcake nightgown I quietly made my way downstairs to investigate. Bill had my mom bent over backwards at the kitchen sink with his hands around her neck. Horrified, I grabbed a fork from the dish strainer and stabbed him right in the ass, yelling, "You leave my mommy alone!"

Stunned, Bill turned around and snapped, "Go back to bed, Jenny!"

Scared, I ran back to my room, got into bed and hugged my teddy bear as tightly as I could. I laid there waiting, wondering if the fighting would continue. I couldn't help but cringe a little when a shadow entered the doorway. Was Bill coming to punish me? My body relaxed as soon as I saw that it was my mom.

"You still awake, honey?" she asked as she sat on the edge of my bed. "It's late. You should be sleeping."

Gently brushing the hair from my face, Mom bent down and kissed my forehead. "I know you were trying to help me, Jenny, but I'm okay. Thank you for coming to my rescue, but I'm a strong lady and I can take that 'Big Bad Billy D'," she said with her arms flexed. I knew she was just trying to make me laugh to ease my fear.

The next day, James and I were outside teaching ourselves how to ride the two-wheeler bicycles we had gotten for Christmas. As usual, Mom and Bill were inside sleeping. The elderly couple next door was sitting on their porch. After watching me fall repeatedly as I attempted to steady myself on the bike, the old man came over and offered to help me. Excited to be receiving some help and attention, I eagerly agreed. He walked briskly alongside me as he held onto the bike, keeping it steady. When the handlebars stopped wobbling back and forth and I was able to hold them straight, he let go and told me to keep peddling.

That nice man spent the entire afternoon teaching James and me how to ride our bikes. Throughout the day he'd ask me questions about what I liked to do, my favorite class in school and other seemingly innocent subjects. At one point he asked me about Mom and Bill.

"I heard a lot of commotion at your house last night," he said as he helped me up off the ground from my latest fall. "Is everything okay?"

I shrugged nonchalantly and said, "Oh that was just my mom and Bill. Sometimes they fight."

"Where are they now?"

"Sleeping. They stay up late at night. Can we try again? I know I'll get it this time?" I was determined to learn to ride that bike by the end of the day.

After that, the old man and I chatted about all kinds of things. He was nice and made me feel comfortable. His wife even brought us lemonade at one point and told me what a pretty little girl I was and what a beautiful smile I had. It was a perfect afternoon. By dinnertime, I was walking on air because I was able to ride a two-wheeler. I couldn't wait until my mom woke up so I could show her.

The next day when I came home from school I could tell that Bill was furious about something. Before I could even put my pink knapsack down, he grabbed me by both arms and started shaking me.

"You little shit!" he screamed. "Don't you *ever* tell anyone what goes on in this house!"

I was too stunned to be scared. Bill raised his hand and just when he was about to smack me across the face, my mom stepped in and sucker-punched him, screaming, "If you ever touch one of my kids again, I'll kill you, Billy."

She pulled me away from him and bent down. Wrapping her arms around me, she held me tight. At that point I started to cry.

Ignoring her, Bill glared at me and with his finger pointing in my face said, "You keep your damn mouth shut about this family, you hear me?"

When he left, I turned to my mom. "I'm sorry," I said through sniffles. "I wasn't telling on him."

Cupping my face in her hands, my mom wiped away my tears. "I know you didn't mean to, sweetie. It's just that some things that happen in our family are private."

"I'm sorry," I said again, hoping Bill wouldn't come back in.

"I love you, baby," Mom said as she gave me a big hug. "You're a good girl and you help Mommy a lot." With that and a kiss on the cheek, all was well in my world again.

Apparently, the elderly gentlemen had come by and told Bill that he was concerned with James and I being left alone during the day while he and mom slept.

Once James and I were able to ride our bikes we hung out with the big kids in the neighborhood everyday, exploring various places in town. We became less of a nuisance to them and more like a little brother and sister. This was the beginning of our introduction to things that usually came much later in life. Instead of sitting home playing with Barbie dolls and GI Joes, my brother and I were gallivanting around town with kids twice our age.

Joey, one of the big kids, became very protective of James and me. One time, when a couple of tough guys who lived on the other side of town knocked James off his bike and tried to force him to do heroin, it was Joey and his friends who chased them away. I'll never forget the time we were hanging out in the basement of Joey's house and he kissed me on the lips. We were lying on an old plaid couch and he told me never to pose for playboy magazine. To this day, I have no idea why he said that to me but will always remember him as being my "first kiss."

When his older brother committed suicide, his tight-knit Italian family fell apart. Joey turned to my mom for comfort and would often come over to our house to talk with her. Mom was always very compassionate and enjoyed helping people. She was very good at giving advice and there were times when I would walk into the kitchen to find her hugging Joey while he wept.

Even though the big kids in the neighborhood were protective of us they were still teenager's and taught us things, like how to embezzle money from Bill, who always had an abundance of cash on hand. He'd pull a wad out of his pocket and give me a fifty dollar bill to go down to the corner market and buy a gallon of milk. In the beginning I would come home, put the milk in the refrigerator and lay the change on the kitchen counter. It was the big kids who made me realize that I could keep the change and Bill would never miss it. Eventually they convinced me to steal money from Bill's pants when he was sleeping so they could use the money to buy porno magazines and cigarettes. James and I did this, not because we were bad but because the "cool" kids told us to and we wanted to be just like them. The more we did these sorts of things, the more they'd let us hang out with them.

While living on Webster Court had its trying times, we did typical kid things, too. All the neighborhood kids would swim in the quarry in the woods near our house—everyone else except me, that is. There were rumors about cars and dead people in that quarry and I swore I would never, ever go in that water. Dead Man's Hill was another place nearby where we would hang out and go sledding in the winter. The rumor was that someone had died going down the hill, giving it its name. It was close to a water tower, which we eventually got the nerve to climb. It was incredible at the top because you could see all of Stoneham and Wakefield from up there. We could even see families sledding down Dead Man's Hill in the winter. Being little kids and all, we felt like we were on top of the world!

I don't know if my mom ever knew where we were all day or what we were doing. As I look back, now, I'm horrified to know that we were so young and spent so much time exploring, being places we shouldn't have been. It was the '70s, however, and a much freer time. Kids could go off for hours to play without parents worrying, something kids today could never do. But despite all our freedom growing up, I always felt loved and cared for. My mom was always there to put a Band-Aid on a scraped knee or cut the crust off my peanut butter and jelly sandwich, even if I had to wake her up to do it. It didn't matter what the day brought, I always knew at the end of it I would be tucked safely in my bed. It was a ritual almost every night. Mom would come to tuck me in, and as she bent over to kiss my forehead her hair would fall into my face, tickling my nose. Sometimes we would have "cuddle time." My mom would crawl into bed with me and I'd lay my head on her chest. The sound of her heartbeat made me feel safe as we talked about many different things. It was those moments that made all the awful stuff seem not so bad.

It may sound hypocritical to be talking about my mom's lifestyle of drugs and parties and yet still say that I loved and admired her. Even though I knew about her cocaine use, except for seeing remnants, I never physically saw her do anything other then smoke pot. Mom and Bill did the most of their partying late at night after we were in bed. From the outside looking in, you might think she was irresponsible and that we should have been taken away from her. But even in the throws of her bad decision-making, I knew how much my mom loved us.

Life on Webster Court didn't affect me negatively because I really didn't know any different. "Normal" is what you know, and I thought everybody's parents partied all night and slept all day. Looking back, I realize that it was that generation's way of forgetting the horrors of the war and upheaval going on around them, as well as, the effects and consequences of the changes and carefree lifestyle they fought so hard to attain. It truly was a different world back then.

After a couple years of living in a haze of drugs, my mom became tired of her life of nonstop partying and needed a change. Realizing that his addictive ways would lose him the love of his life, Bill decided to buy a secluded piece of property in a little town called Wentworth in the White Mountains of New Hampshire. They would start a new life away from the city and its temptations. It would be a chance to start fresh and have the life my mother dreamed of, and maybe even change the restless soul she saw in Bill.

For years to come, Mom's family and friends would question her choice to make a life with this man.

Chapter Three

The yellow Volkswagen Bug wound its way up the dirt road that was just wide enough for a car to pass through and obviously very much neglected. With Mom and Bill in the front and James and I in the back, we drove for what seemed like an hour past rundown houses and farms and a brook that ran, at times, alongside the road.

Finally we arrived at our new home. Mom was a little skeptical, but she knew that living in New Hampshire was what was best for everyone. The five and a half acres of mostly raw land that Bill purchased for $20,000 flanked the road. A little house was nestled on one side and the shell of a much larger log house lay at the crest of the horseshoe-shaped driveway. The little house was nothing more than a two-bedroom shack with a living room, kitchen and non-functioning bathroom. The house lacked plumbing and running water, so James and I had to lug five-gallon buckets of water up a 100-foot incline from the river across the road to the house. But it was home, and the piece of relatively untouched nature represented new beginnings.

By then, James was seven and I was eight and Mom thought growing up in the country would be better and safer for all of us. She knew it was her only chance to get away from what had become her life: non-stop partying, being up all night, sleeping all day, going from one "good time" to another. My mom quickly became excited about the prospects of this new life and started making plans for the main house.

James and I enjoyed our new life as well. We were never without something to do, and spent our days exploring every inch of our wilderness playground. We swam, fished and bathed in the same brook from which we had to lug water up to the house for cooking and washing. We made forts and hiding places in the woods amongst the fallen trees and huge rocks. With our blond hair and closeness in age, we could have almost passed for twins—except that James has brown eyes and mine are blue, and his thin hair was styled in a bowl-cut and mine was the texture of an afro without the curl. "Pubic hair," Bill called it. Most days I looked as if I'd stuck my finger in a light socket. People often commented that they'd never seen hair like that before.

We were especially happy when Nard and Linda moved to New Hampshire with their kids, who were like siblings to us. Nard and her son Shawn, who was six months younger than I, moved into a mobile home in the next town, about eight miles from the farm. She, too, had started to see that the life she was living in the city was leading her down the wrong path and needed a change. Nard wanted a brighter future and started making plans to go to college.

Linda and her daughter Becky, who was a year younger than James, moved into a log cabin a few miles from the farm. Still having a difficult time dealing with her "situation" as a teenager, Linda continued to use substances heavily to ease the pain. She also still harbored some jealousy toward my mom and Bill (Linda was dating him first). Mom knew that Linda hadn't completely gotten over the rejection and was extremely considerate of her feelings. Although Linda had divorced Tommy a few years prior she was still very much co-dependent on men and quickly met a local Vietnam Veteran named Doug and married him.

Bill had started construction on the main house. He had lots of friends, from members of the "Hells Angels"—a badass motorcycle gang from Massachusetts—to people he met in the "business" along the way. His personality projected power and Bill was always able to entice his friends to help out around the farm. Whenever he needed something done, Bill knew someone who could do it for very little, if any, money. When he wanted the land cleared, graded and extensively landscaped, he got some people from

Vermont to bring in their heavy equipment on the weekends for a "working party." I called them the "friends and freaks of the farm." (It wasn't until I became a teenager that I learned just how freaky they were.)

Bill even made us a makeshift teeter-totter out of scrap wood using a two-by-four and a twenty-gallon plastic bucket filled with concrete to keep it from tipping over. It was great fun until one day Bill decided to use it with us. As soon as he sat on the wood, it catapulted James into the air before hitting the ground. I guess Bill forgot that his 250 pounds was no match for a seven-year-old who weighed less than seventy pounds soaking wet. Fortunately, James ended up with only a few scrapes and cuts, but Bill couldn't stop talking about it.

"Did you see the f****** air that kid caught? That was cool!" Bill said, unconcerned if James was hurt or not. Mom went over and gently picked James up and carried him into the house where she cleaned and bandaged his elbow and knee.

Over the next year, things began to mellow somewhat. Mom and Bill had a son they named Jason. He was the pride and joy of the whole family and another example of my mom's hope for the future. She was happy to see that the life she'd chosen in the country had given her children back the innocence the city had taken away. The main house, which had once been a hollow shell, was turned into a three-bedroom, two-bathroom log home with a finished basement, a stone hearth with wood-burning stove, and all new appliances and modern conveniences. Bill had to have the best of everything, and everything had to be done on the grandest scale. He utilized the "open concept" and combined the kitchen, living room, and dining room. The final touch was a huge wraparound porch with built-in seats. It became Bill's perch as he could survey every inch of the property from it. For the first time in my life, I had my own bedroom.

Mom designed the gardens directly behind the main house. Down the steps off the porch, a grape trellis hung over the stone walkway leading to a rose garden that surrounded the house on the right and a small herb garden (both legal and illegal) on the left. On the other side of the roses was a hill that descended to a man-made pond, complete with gazebo. In the summertime, Bill would stock the pond with trout for fishing, and in the winter we used it to ice skate. Bill bought four-wheelers and dirt bikes to get around the grounds. The farm had become a "community" that we rarely had to leave.

While the men busied themselves building and remodeling, Mom taught James and me how to plant and care for the rose and herb garden. Since moving to the mountains, she had become interested in the organic, natural way of life. She wanted everything to be pure and wholesome for her children. Gone were the days when James and I wandered freely around the city while Mom and Bill slept. Gone were the late-night parties and drug-induced fights. Now we worked and played together like any other family, or so I thought. The only thing I knew Mom continued to indulge in was marijuana, but so was the rest of the country. Mom would say, "Even those who won't admit they smoke pot do."

With her long hair pulled back in a loose clip and a red bandana tied around her head, Mom would don her Levi overalls and head out to her favorite place, the garden, every evening after dinner. It wasn't as hot at that time of day, and Mom said that watering after the sun started to go down was better because it had more time to soak into the soil. James was a real Mama's boy. When he wasn't helping me pull weeds he was attached to Mom and would often be seen hugging her leg with his head resting on her hip. Meanwhile Jason, nicknamed "Buff" because he liked to run around naked, wanted to help in the garden too. Mom would take him to the corner of the garden and tell him to dig a hole so she could plant some more seeds. The task would keep him busy for a few minutes, but then, like a typical toddler, he'd get right back into mischief again.

Tending to the garden became our ritual and I savored every moment shared with my mom after we moved to New Hampshire. She and I had some of our best conversations during that time. We would talk about life and what she believed in, her philosophies. Mom didn't conform to the ways of life that most people did. She believed in peace through love and tolerance. We had some serious talks about subjects that usually ended with her telling me, "You will understand what I mean someday." Like when I asked her why she stayed with Bill even when he was so mean to her.

Mom was polite and accepting of everyone, which is probably why she was loved and respected by so many people.

"Loving means accepting others as they are and not judging them by their differences," she would tell me when I would comment on some of the freaks who hung out at the house. Her simple explanations always seemed to satisfy me and I believed that when the day came she would be there to explain further, just as she'd said.

Dinner was something else that became a real family affair once we moved to New Hampshire. Bill was a meat- and-potatoes kind of guy and always wanted a hearty meal at the end of his hardworking day. Every night we literally had a seven-course meal, and whoever happened to be living or working at the farm was invited to stay. The only part of this tradition the kids weren't included in was their after-dinner "dessert." We got ice cream, but the grownups got something else. While Mom cleaned up the dishes, Bill would retreat to the living room and "twist up a fatty." The grownups would sit around and smoke the joint while we kids ran around and played. Smoking was always done in the open, so it really meant nothing to us. It was just the way it was. Like I've said before, normal is what you know, and I didn't know any different. (Looking back now, I realize it had a huge impact on who I am today and my beliefs about certain subjects.)

In the spring of 1980, when I turned ten, Bill bought a motorcycle. One warm day, we took a ride down the dirt road toward a campground situated along the Baker River. While passing some bikers who were setting up camp, Bill made the peace sign. A typical gesture made to fellow bikers. On our way back home we passed the bikers again only this time they had formed a human roadblock, forcing us to stop. I'm not sure what the argument was about, but it became very heated. Just as I sensed it was getting bad I saw my mom standing behind them with a shotgun in her hand.

"Get the f--- away from my old man!" she yelled, pointing the gun right at the men.

The bikers backed off, saying, "We don't have a beef. It's cool." They moved aside and we went on our way.

When we got back to the farm, Bill grabbed the gun from my mom and said, "What did you think you were going to do with this, Patty?"

"I was defending my family," she said, annoyed that he was questioning her intentions.

"There's no shell in it and the safety button's on. It wouldn't have done you any good if they'd called your bluff."

"Oh well, they didn't know that," she said with a shrug and walked away. Over her shoulder she yelled, "It served its purpose, didn't it?"

"Always a smart-ass, Patty," Bill hollered back.

Even I knew that Bill was trying to show Mom the seriousness of the situation, but she just figured everything turned out okay so what's the big deal.

Most of that summer was spent at the lake. Mom would pack us kids up in her little VW Bug and take us to Stinson Lake to go swimming. Not far from the farm, it was her favorite spot and she would bring a picnic lunch of peanut butter and jelly sandwiches and Kool-Aid and we would spend the whole day there. James always seemed to have a permanent red mustache across his top lip from guzzling cups of Hawaiian Punch Kool-Aid. Almost always, Nard and Linda and their kids would come with us. The Moms would sit on the shore sunbathing and smoking Old Gold filter cigarettes while we kids frolicked in the water. Sometimes, on extremely hot days, the men would take a break from working on the farm and come to the lake and go swimming too. Having no shred of modesty, they often skinny-dipped. They were hippies and believed a naked body was a beautiful and natural way of expression.

In August we went to an outside music festival in Vermont. It was like a mini Woodstock with different bands playing over the course of three days. We camped out in a tent. One of our beloved dogs, White Cloud, had had puppies a couple of months earlier and Bill made us bring them to the festival and told James and me to try and give them away. James, sporting denim shorts and I, wearing a navy-blue halter top and red shorts, wandered around the festival, each holding one of the seven-week-old German Sheppard pups. Inevitably people would come up to us and say, "Oh, how cute! Can I hold it?"

"Sure," we would eagerly respond. "You can have it." After handing the pup over, we'd run off into the crowd and go get another puppy. There were hundreds of people at this festival, and we gave away all five pups, rather deceptively.

While we were at the music festival, we saw a group of young girls at a table doing Tarot card and palm readings.

"Mommy, I want to have my palm read," I said, tugging at her skirt.

"I don't think so honey, you don't want to know what your future holds," she said sternly.

"But I want to know what I'm going to be when I grow up," I persisted.

"Life is what you make of it, Jenny. You must enjoy each day because it could all be gone in the blink of an eye," she said adamantly.

I suspect that statement came from her palm-reading experience in San Francisco. Mom didn't get mad at us very often, but I could tell by the stern tone in her voice that she was serious and not even one of my temper tantrums would get me my way.

With the main house complete, Bill quickly financed major construction on the rest of the property. A massive barn had been built at the bottom of the south entrance. It was a 150 x 100-foot, two-story building with a concrete floor and two bays. The first floor stored all the trucks and farming equipment and also housed an office and bathroom. Stairs tucked in a corner zigzagged to the top floor where there was a large open space with closets on all four corners. The brass handles on every door were kept locked at all times. He didn't want anyone stealing his "expensive power tools," or so he said.

The grounds soon filled with all the necessary equipment needed to run a farm. Bill purchased the adjacent property for $60,000. About three-quarters of a mile from the farm and over 100 acres, the "property" would eventually be a place of great significance. It had an area affectionately called "Thailand," a place we prayed no one would ever find because it held the "other" larger herb garden. On that part of the property was a pond the size of a small lake. Bill brought the "Vermont people" back to build a road leading to it and named it Pelican Point.

Our two dogs, White Cloud, a pure white German Sheppard and Pelican, an Irish Setter, were our best companions. They were good dogs and made sure James and I were safe, following us everywhere we went. Usually whenever the dogs followed someone out to the property, they would come right back. But one time they didn't, and after a couple of days Bill went out looking for them. While walking up the road toward the property, he found Pelican dead from a bullet hole through his neck, most likely from a hunting accident. White Cloud was never found, but we suspected the same bullet also hit him as they often ran side by side and he likely wandered off somewhere to die.

That year, Bill also bought a Kubota tractor and bucket loader valued at over $200,000. He always paid cash for everything, insisting that he didn't trust banks. In fact, one time during the construction of the farm, Bill went into the Pemigewasset Bank with around $20,000 in cash and wanted to trade it in for larger, crisper bills. When the bank teller saw how mildewed the currency was, she refused to accept it. I don't know the final outcome of that situation; I just remember Bill ranting and raving about how ridiculous it was that they wouldn't exchange the money. In his arrogant mind there was no reason good enough why the bank shouldn't have taken that money; dirty, mildewed or not, and exchange it for something cleaner.

"Money is money," he complained, standing in the middle of the driveway with his usual audience (he loved being the center of attention). "It all spends the same. "What'a f****** retard."

That was Bill's favorite expression. He had a very short fuse and zero tolerance for idiocy. Of course, to him everyone was an idiot, therefore everyone was an F****** retard.

Still, thanks to Bill, the once small, five-and-a-half-acre plot with two shanty-like buildings blossomed into a valuable estate of over 100 acres, capable of operating as a full-fledged farm. The little house we lived in when we first moved to New Hampshire was remodeled, refurbished and expanded to become a "staff house" for employees who worked on the farm or for overnight guests who needed a place to crash.

Everything felt right; it was a new beginning for all of us. No one could have predicted this was the beginning of a life of more horror and tragedy than any of us could imagine.

Chapter Four

Bill continued to be involved in the "driftwood" business, which I know was somewhat true because we had a lot of primitive-looking furniture throughout the house. But even fatherhood wasn't enough to keep him home. He had an insatiable appetite for danger and risk-taking. He needed the adrenalin rush that he felt from life in the city and the day-to-day game of survival.

"I'm off to slay the dragon," he would say before he left.

In an attempt to make up for his extended leaves, Bill would shower Mom with gifts. He'd bring her the most beautiful dresses and jewelry from the many exotic places around the world he visited. I believe Bill wanted to be a better person and lead a normal life for my mom, but all he knew were the streets and the life he made on them. Eventually, Mom conceded that she could take the man out of the city but she couldn't take the city out of the man.

I'm almost positive that my mom was the love of Bill's life, but at the same time he also thrived on the risk that came with cheating. Bill always had to have the companionship of a woman on his long trips. When my mother couldn't go, he would bring someone else. Bill was never without a woman, in fact, he cheated on the girlfriends that he cheated on my Mom with. One was a waitress from his favorite restaurant "The Tenney Mountain Steak Barn." Her name was Carry and she was the daughter of the Chief of Police in the town where we lived. For a long time, Mom didn't know about Carry. Bill was very good at keeping certain aspects of his life hidden. In fact, he had been messing around with Carry even before we moved to New Hampshire, which was probably the main reason he always had to come up north to "check on the property." But as with most lies, they eventually were revealed. I vividly recall the day my mom found out about Carry.

Sometimes at nine o'clock at night, Bill would decide he was hungry and wanted to go to "The Steak Barn" for something to eat. Whoever happened to be at the farm would always be invited (he was very generous in that way) so we often had a large crowd. Mom would herd us three little kids out to the car, half asleep and more often than not in our pajamas. Bill was a regular at the restaurant and always sat at the same big round table in the corner. The windows were floor-to-ceiling and overlooked the Baker River. My little brother Jason was always intrigued by the view and would stand in front of the window banging on it. James and I would usually pull up a piece of the orange shag carpet and lie down next to the table and go back to sleep.

But this particular night I stayed up.

It seemed that Carry was always working when we went there (usually two or three times a week), but she was never our waitress. Bill always invented a reason to go into the kitchen to see the cook or make a phone call. On this particular night, however, Carry came over to our table and started oohing and aahing over my little brother Jason.

Bill, who often flirted with women, said, "Well, if you ever want to have a good-looking kid, you know where to come."

Mom must have noticed the difference in Bill's flirtatiousness that night. She shot him a look that said, "We will discuss this when we get home." Carry obviously sensed the sudden tension between Mom and Bill because she quickly left the table. Mom had a conniption when her suspicions were later founded. Shortly after that night she found proof that Bill had been cheating on her with Carry and that he had even bedded her at the farm. After that, Mom didn't want anything to do with the farm and told Bill she was moving out.

"There's no way I'm sleeping in the same room you screwed that chick in," she screamed.

Mom packed whatever she could fit in her VW Bug, along with my brothers and me. She had threatened to leave Bill many times in the past but this time I really thought it was for real. Unfortunately, she only drove out one end of the driveway and back in the other. I've often wondered how different my life would have been if she had kept going that night.

As usual, Bill continued to make broken promises, swearing to stop fooling around and professing his love to her. The very next day, after Moms attempted break-up, he made plans to add a new master bedroom. Bill hired some people to rip off the roof and put on a whole new floor. Being the eccentric person that he is, Bill had the king-size bed, dressers and nightstands built into the wall. He included a huge walk-in closet (with removable floor boards) and a master bath. An enormous spiral staircase went from the new master bedroom through to the first floor and down to the basement. Bill did everything he could to please my mom and it worked for awhile.

Soon Mom realized that her financial security came with a price, and she was forced to turn a blind eye to Bill's continued infidelities. After seven years of being with him she grew tired of it but knew he would never change. The alternative, life as a single parent wasn't very appealing either. Mom decided that her way of dealing with Bill's cheating was to go out and screw around with somebody else. One night, while Bill was away on "business," Mom, Nard, Linda and Karen (another one of my mom's childhood friends who moved to New Hampshire) went out dancing, something they did often and always at Bill's expense. Mom knew that Bill had some chick with him again, so she brought a guy home with her. I woke up and heard them going at it on the living room couch.

The next morning I called her on it and she said, "Jenny, we are girls, and sometimes we will have secrets between us. This is one of those times. Someday you'll understand what I'm doing." (It took me twenty years to realize exactly what she was doing: having "revenge sex." And it had a significant effect on my life.)

As I look back I don't think my mom was unhappy then, but I don't think she was all that happy, either. The life she'd chosen with Bill was the lesser of two evils.

Chapter Five

With the farm growing and at least five people working for him, Bill felt comfortable going off on longer "business trips". Sometimes he would be gone for weeks at a time. Alvin was his foremen, his right-hand man. He made sure that Mom had everything she needed and that the farm was running smoothly while Bill was away. We called him "Uncle Al." Linda's husband Doug and Karen's husband Peter where employed to do most of the carpentry and mechanical jobs around the farm. Nard and Linda helped in the vegetable gardens, which spanned about two football fields on the north side of the main house. Bill hired a guy named Steven "Suds" Sudvari as a farmhand to do odd jobs around the farm.

In his early twenties, Suds had moved to the area with his girlfriend Kathy from Pennsylvania. They rented an apartment in town next door to Linda and Doug, who vouched for his character; he even passed "Bills test" and was deemed trustworthy.

Bill liked to play mind games with people, test their loyalty and their greed. He would put them in situations where they were alone with valuable things like money or the key to locked rooms. I don't know what happened to those who didn't pass, or if anyone had ever failed but Suds quickly became a loyal employee and friend to Mom and Bill.

Suds was a quiet guy who mostly kept to himself but was always around to help when needed. He even used to baby-sit my brothers and me on occasion. I remember a time in early October, 1980, when the trees were turning a beautiful mix of red, yellow and orange. Mom had called the farm and asked Suds to bring me to Nard's house, where she was. Halfway there, his car broke down and we had to walk the remaining half-mile.

Wearing dirty blue jeans, cowboy boots and a jean jacket over a pale yellow T-shirt Suds' presence made the hairs on the back of my neck stand up that day. His handlebar mustache hid the fact that he was missing three of his top front teeth, and his long brown hair hung in his face, hiding his vacant eyes. (That was one thing I really remember about him. When you looked into his eyes, they were dull, almost dead-like.) That day, I walked on the opposite side of the road from him because I was so creeped out. All he talked about the whole way to Nard's was his girlfriend Kathy. They were having problems, and he thought she was going to leave him. I don't know why Suds was telling me, a ten-year-old, all about his problems with his relationship.

No one likes an unhappy person, I thought to myself. It was something I often heard Mom say to Bill when he was complaining and wished I had the nerve to say it to Suds.

Mom liked Suds though. She seemed to have a soft spot for him, especially after Kathy left him a month later. She knew a lot about his past and tried to help him through it with words of encouragement. She always made a concerted effort to speak to him kindly and let him know how much she appreciated everything he did around the farm. She made sure to include him in the tight circle of friends she and Bill had in an effort to make him feel a part of the family.

Noticing that Suds was depressed and more easily aggravated, Mom realized that Kathy's departure had affected him greatly. He was very angry, and feelings of hatred had resurfaced. Things got worse when Suds contacted his probation officer in Pennsylvania and found out there was a warrant out for his arrest. He had failed to pay a fine of restitution on an incident that had occurred a few years before he moved to New Hampshire.

Thinking that perhaps the breakup with Kathy and his legal problems had ignited post-traumatic stress from his time in Vietnam, Mom helped Suds find a support group for veterans. She found one in Manchester, New Hampshire and even made the initial contact on his behalf. Suds attended a few sessions but then gave it up when he was told there was nothing they could do about his legal matters in Pennsylvania. "It's nothing but a waste of my time," He spat one night when Mom asked him how his meeting went.

When I asked why she was taking such an interest in helping Suds, Mom said, "Suds is a lost soul trying to find some connection in life. He's had some really sad things happen to him and I just want to help him."

"Like what?" I asked curiously.

"Well, his mommy died when he was only six years old. Can you imagine growing up without me?"

That brought tears to my eyes and I started to cry—not for Suds, but at the thought of my mom dying.

"Suds needs a friend right now," Mom continued. "With Kathy gone he has no one."

I was haunted for the rest of the day by this conversation and had nightmares about it for months. But I was a little more sympathetic towards Suds after that. Each time I saw him, I would picture him as a little boy without a mom and it would make me very sad and whenever Bill would yell at him I felt bad.

Bill's only involvement with Suds was to give him chores to do around the farm, treating him like he treated most people, dismissively. Mom made it a point to converse with him on a more respectable level. They often got into some interesting and deep conversations, once regarding, of all things, the War on Drugs campaign. Drugs were still prevalent throughout the country not just on the farm where I lived. Richard Nixon had declared the war on drugs in 1976, stating that "drugs were public enemy number one." But it was the Reagan administration that vamped it up with First Lady, Nancy Reagan's campaign "Just Say No" using an advertisement with fried eggs and the slogan "This is your brain - This is your brain on drugs."

Mom was a liberal and very vocal about how she felt about marijuana. She thought it should be legalized, as did everyone else who hung out at the farm. Interestingly, Suds revealed how it was the military who supplied the harder, more psychedelic drugs to soldiers while they were in Vietnam. He shared with my mom how he had become addicted to heroin while he was over there. This ignited an intense discussion about how hypocritical the government and politicians were and that anything "organized" was clearly backed by propaganda. When Ronald Reagan won presidency in November 1980 I remember walking into the kitchen and seeing "REAGAN FOR PRESIDENT – BUMMER!" written on the blackboard in big, bold letters.

When Christmas arrived that year, as usual, we spent Christmas Eve in Massachusetts, first at Bill's parents' house and then at Nana and Pa's, Mom's parents. Mom always looked so nice and loved dressing up for special occasions. Her long hair was tied up in a French twist and she wore a blue-and-white floral dress and high heels. Even Bill cleaned up pretty nicely, dressed in a suit jacket and tie. I wore a black velvet skirt and silver silk shirt with black patent leather shoes. Mom even managed to do something with my rebellious hair, tying it back with a red clip. My little brothers were dressed up in suits and ties.

Having grown up in a strict Catholic family, it was expected that we attend midnight mass with the family. Mom knew it made Nana happy so she endured the hour-long service for her sake. It wasn't that my mom didn't believe in God; she just didn't practice it the way the rest of her family did (except her brother Skippy, who was a hippie, too). She was a nonconformist, which was perhaps one of the reasons there was a bridge between her and my grandparents. Still, Mom was always respectful of them and their values.

After church we headed back up north so we could be home for Christmas morning. My brothers and I slept in the back of the car and were carried in one by one by Bill. After tucking us into bed to await Santa's arrival, Bill and Mom put out all the presents. Our quilted, square patch stockings that Mom had made hung on the mantle above the woodstove and were filled with candy and trinkets. That year I got a Magic 8 ball.

"So you can predict your own future," Mom said with a chuckle.

"Neat," I said, knowing it was in relation to my asking her if I could have my palm read at the festival over the summer.

The next present I opened contained a thumb-sucking, furry doll that looked like a monkey. It was called a Monchichi. Bill, who was sitting on the sofa, started laughing and announced, "When I saw that thing in the store with all that wild hair, all I could think about was how much it looked like you."

Sitting on the floor amidst all the colorful wrapping paper strewn everywhere, my mouth pinched shut and eyes narrowed, I glared at Bill. He thought it was hysterical, but I didn't think it was very funny. He knew I hated my hair. "You're just a big jerk, you meany," I snapped at him as he continued to laugh.

"Oh, Jenny, he was only kidding," Mom said, trying to avoid the fight she saw coming. "Here, open something else."

After we were finished opening all our gifts, James went off to try out his new Magic Rock Garden, and Jason, who was now two and a half years old, sat in the middle of the living room playing with his Matchbox Stunt Track. Bill crawled onto the floor to play with him.

Mom busied herself cleaning the house and cooking while my brothers and I played with our new toys. The one thing about my mom that has always stuck with me is how she always hummed when she cleaned or cooked or was concentrating on something. It was as if she always enjoyed whatever it was she was doing, even household chores.

It was the best Christmas I had ever had, and one I will never forget.

Chapter Six

By the end of February 1981, Bill was off on another "business trip". James and I would spend our school vacation with our dad in Massachusetts. It would be our first time away from Mom for any length of time and a whole week seemed like a lifetime to me. My dad was a virtual stranger to us and I didn't relish staying with him for so long. I tried relentlessly to make Mom feel guilty and keep us home instead, but it didn't work. She had plans of her own.

Driving south on Interstate 93, I fought back tears as loneliness weighed heavily on my heart. Still struggling with the fear of Mom dying, the enormity of these thoughts had sent me sobbing into her room most nights. She would rock me, her arms wrapped lovingly around my body. I would feel safe and secure when she'd say, "Jenny, dying is a part of living and you can't live in fear of it." She'd reassure me that she wasn't going to die any time soon and I had nothing to worry about. Cuddled in the crest of her arm, I would fall back asleep while she stroked my hair and hummed a soft melody.

I tried to be strong as we pulled up to the curb in front of my dad's house. I knew Mom was glad to hand over some of the responsibility to him for a change, but I was still not one bit happy about this and prayed the week would go by fast.

At least we'll get to see Nana and Pa, I thought.

Everything in Dad's apartment was old and cheap—from the Budweiser mirror that hung on the wall (probably won at some county fair) to the mismatched plaid furniture in the living room and the shag rug that reeked of spilled beer and cigarettes. The dingy red curtains hanging over the front window were closed, making the room seem dark and depressing, even in daylight.

A strange feeling of dread came over me.

"I love you, my number one son," Mom said to James as she got ready to leave.

He was hugging her leg and crying because he, too, didn't want her to go.

She bent down and gave him a big kiss and said, "It's okay. You'll have fun with Daddy. And sissy will be here with you." She tousled James' hair and made her way toward the door.

I went over and gave her a hug and kiss good-bye. "Promise you'll call us every night," I said, swallowing hard so the tears would stay back.

"I promise, Jenny. You be good for your dad, and make sure to help him with James."

"I will," I promised and hugged her tighter than ever before, inhaling the familiar scent of her hair that fell in my face as she bent down to hug me back.

"I'll see you next weekend," Mom said as she walked toward the car, waving behind her. "I love you, Jenny" were the last words she said before she drove away.

No longer able to contain my tears, I let them spill freely down my cheeks.

After Mom dropped us off, she headed back to the farm in New Hampshire. Nard had driven down with her to drop us off. Suds was at the farm babysitting Jason. Bill was on a vessel in Wale City, Bermuda, which, unbeknownst to Mom, was being seized for having marijuana and hash oil.

Knowing that Bill had yet again taken some chick with him on his "business trip," Mom was furious when she said to Nard, "Billy doesn't go anywhere alone. He needs constant reassurance from women that he's number one. Well, he can have them because I'm all done."

"I don't know how you've put up with it all these years, Patty," Nard replied, shaking her head as she lit up a joint.

"Me neither, but screw that. I'm not gonna forgive him. Not this time," Patty said, taking the joint from Nard. "I'm fed up. I'm tired of looking the other way, I don't deserve to be treated this way and what the hell kind of message am I sending my kids."

For the next hour as they drove north, Patty let out all her frustrations about Bill and his lifestyle. Nard was a good friend, always there, always supportive and encouraging. She and Patty had been through a lot during their years of friendship and could always count on one another.

"I could do it on my own," Patty said, still talking about leaving Bill. "I have my nursing degree…it's not like I can't get a good job. In fact, I've wanted to work in Hanover at Dartmouth Hitchcock ever since we moved to New Hampshire, but Bill would never let me. He said I didn't need to work."

"I know you can Patty," Nard said encouragingly. "And I will help you out with the kids, watch them when you have to work." Deep down inside Nard knew that nothing good could ever come of Patty and Bills relationship. But she would never tell her friend that. All she could do was support whatever choice Patty made. But from the tone in Patty's voice, Nard truly believed she was serious this time and that she would actually leave Bill.

We had arrived at Dad's on a Saturday. The next day, he piled James and me in the back of his Ford Vista and drove over the state line into New Hampshire so he could buy beer. (You couldn't purchase alcohol in Massachusetts on Sundays. Why he hadn't thought ahead and stocked up the day before, I'll never know.) Over the course of the next few days, Dad did his best to entertain us. We went bowling—rather, James and I bowled, while Dad sat and drank. We also went to Dad's favorite place, The Italian American Club. James and I played pool for hours while he sat at the bar and got drunk. I even had to call someone to give us a ride home because Dad was too drunk to drive. I remember thinking; *I'm only ten years old and have already been taking care of James for years. Now I have to take care of my dad, too.*

On Thursday, we awoke to about a foot of snow. The entire east coast had been buried by a Nor'easter, but we still went for a scheduled visit to my maternal grandparents' house. Nana and Pa lived in the same town of Wakefield about five minutes away from my dad's house, but their house was in the upper middle class part of town adjacent to a baseball field and playground. James and I loved to go to our grandparents' house, as there was always something fun to do. They had a large three-bedroom house with a finished basement that had been turned into a little apartment. (We lived there for a while after my mom left my dad.)

Pa, an oil burner repair man, had been very savvy at saving and investing his money, so they were financially very comfortable. Every time James and I visited, Pa would pretend to pull a five dollar bill out from behind our ears and give it to us. He loved to joke with us and loved even more being a grandpa. Unlike most women of her era, Nana always worked. She was a secretary for a company called "The Lord Wakefield."

While we were visiting Nana and Pa, Mom called. It was so good to hear her voice, and she was excited to talk to us, too. It made me realize how much I missed her.

"Hey, Mom," I said when Nana handed me the phone.

"Hi, baby girl."

"Did you get all the snow that we did?" I asked excitedly, twisting the phone cord in my fingers.

"We sure did," Mom said. "In fact, we don't have any electricity at the farm right now. We didn't have any last night, either."

"What'd you do?" I asked, pacing back and forth in Nana's kitchen. James was standing in front of me, eagerly awaiting his turn to talk.

"I had a little candlelight dinner party last night. Linda and Doug, and Karen and Peter and Uncle Al and Suds were here."

"Where's Jason?" I asked.

"He's here. I think I'll take him sledding later. What are you kids up to today?"

"Pa said he might take us ice skating," I replied, bummed that I couldn't go sledding with her and my little brother. We had a great hill by the house, and when the snow was packed you could get some great speed. It made me want to go home even more. "I can't wait to come home," I told her, wishing away the time like I had been doing all week.

"Are you having fun?" she asked.

When I told her about all the bar hopping we'd been doing with Dad, I could hear the disappointment in her voice. She sighed and said, "It's only one more day, Jenny. I love you. I'll see you tomorrow."

"I love you, too," I said before handing the phone to James.

The next morning I awoke to the sound of the telephone ringing. It was around 7:30 AM. Excited because today Mom was coming to pick us up, I woke James. I figured it must be Mom on the phone letting my dad know what time she'd arrive. As I lay on the pull-out couch in my father's living room, I could see him in the kitchen. I watched as he stretched the long white phone cord across the room into the bathroom and shut the door. I wondered what he was doing in there for so long. I couldn't hear any water running. When he finally emerged, all he said was, "I have to run out for a minute."

He returned about thirty minutes later with his best friend. James and I were still lying on the couch watching *One Day At A time* on the small black and white TV with a rabbit ear antenna on top. Nothing seemed unusual—not even the sound of a beer can popping open so early in the morning.

It wasn't until my dad called us into the kitchen that I could tell something was wrong. The tone of his voice was different, serious. Usually he was carefree and joking. James and I each sat on one of his knees, facing each other. It was eerie, and I could sense something terrible was about to happen. Dad wasn't able to make eye contact with us. He stared down at the floor with an arm around each of us and said, "There's been an accident. Your mother's had an accident."

Struggling to find the right words, his eyes welled up with tears. He appealed to his friend for moral support. Mustering up what little courage and manhood he possessed, he continued, "I'm afraid she's no longer with us." It was all he could say before he started to weep.

"What does that mean.....no longer with us?"

I'll never forget watching the life go right out of James' eyes as the blood drained from his face. His whole world revolved around our mom and her love. I realized at that moment that our lives would never be the same. Life as we knew it would cease to exist. I was numb as my dad's words echoed over and over in my head.

Oh, please, God, let me wake up from this nightmare. I must be dreaming...this can't be happening...I want to see my mom. What sort of sick joke is this? Where is Jason? What kind of accident?

So many questions ran through my head. But my dad had no answers, no explanations.

Later that day, I laid on the couch in the living room staring out the window. It was February 27, 1981 and I felt like I was looking at life for the first time. In some ways I may have been; it was the first time I was looking at life as a motherless child. The massive snowstorm that had blanketed New England the day before was still evident; the street looked like a winter wonderland. Thousands of people in Massachusetts, New Hampshire, Maine and Vermont were still without electricity. Everything looked cold and dismal as I sat trying to digest the news that my mother was dead. I waited for someone, anyone, to come and see me. I needed something familiar. I waited for Nana and Pa or my aunt, who lived only minutes away, to come over and explain what was happening. I needed to be comforted, to feel some of the love my mother had always given me—which I would never feel again. But no one came. Those were the loneliest two days of my life.

Staying at my dad's place was very strange; in fact, I'd even had a nightmare that my mother was being backed against a wall by a dark figure holding a knife. I never slept well away from home and I just wanted this to all go away. I wanted to wake up from this horrible dream. I hadn't seen my mom in days, and now he was telling me I'd never see her again. The emotions I felt were devastating, and I desperately needed someone to help me make sense of it all. But that never happened. As I waited my heart began to harden. I felt nothing. This is when I taught myself not to feel pain, the walls came slamming down—the shield that would protect me from all the tragic events to come.

Finally Bill arrived with Jason. When he had returned from his "trip," he'd headed straight to the hospital in New Hampshire. Two-and-a-half-year-old Jason had been there since the "accident." When I asked Jason about the bandages on his face, he told me that he'd been cut during the "accident." Distraught about the news of my mom, I was concerned more about the "what" than the "how." I accepted his explanation of an "accident" as we headed over to Nana's house. When we got there, I immediately walked over to the photo of my mom, James and me sitting on the TV. Even though it was a few years old, I stood staring at it. Suddenly, someone came up behind me. As the arms wrapped around me, I realized it was my aunt. It was the first expression of comfort anyone had offered since I'd been told about my mother's death two days earlier.

Later that night, still at my grandparents, my brothers and I sat outside on the porch looking up at the moon. Bill, my dad and Nana and Pa were inside discussing arrangements and the fate of my brothers and me.

Suddenly Jason called out, "Why did the bad man hurt my mommy and make her bleed?"

"What are you talking about?" I asked.

Confused, James and I looked at each other and then at Jason. We'd been told that our mom had been in a car accident.

"Where's Mommy," he continued, ignoring my question.

The sickness and disillusion I already felt was heightened by his outburst and the fact that I had learned the truth about my mom's "accident" from my baby brother. I felt like I'd been kicked in the stomach. Once I had a chance to recover, I focused my attention back on Jason, who had stitches down the entire right side of his face. He was crying and looking to me for answers, but I didn't have any.

Knowing it was up to me to make some sense of all this, to give this baby some peace, I invented the story of "Mommy on the moon." I told him that Mommy was going to live on the moon, that we wouldn't be able to see her or touch her but that we could talk to her and she would be watching over us. (For years after that, we would go out every night and talk to the moon and blow kisses, bidding it good-night! It was somehow comforting to have a visual of where our mom was. To this day, whenever I look at the moon I can't help but think of my mom and imagine her watching over me.)

As we continued to sit out on the porch, the grown-ups argued inside over where we kids would live. I couldn't believe it. We'd just lost our mother, and all they could do was fight! My mother's will stated that all three of her children were to remain together. Jason was Bill's biological son, so there was no question where he would go. My dad couldn't take care of *himself*, much less two kids. Legally, James and I were supposed to go to my mother's sister and her husband, Auntie Mary and Uncle Fred. But that contradicted Mom's will and became the reason for their heated discussion.

Auntie Mary, the youngest of my grandparents' children, had married her college sweetheart. They had two children, Jessica and Justin, thriving careers, and lived with my grandparents to save money. The idea of having three kids dumped on them wasn't part of their idyllic life plan, even though we had seen, and lost, so much at our young ages. Wanting to fulfill my mothers wish, Bill was intent on keeping us together. It was obvious my mom's family didn't want us, but they didn't want Bill to have us, either; they knew the kind of life he led.

With no resolution in sight, Bill took us from my grandparent's on the pretense of buying new clothes. He insisted on getting us a new wardrobe, as well as something for the funeral. As I stared out the car window into traffic, all I could hear was *She's no longer with us*. Feeling numb from shock, I couldn't stop the words from repeating in my head. We went to the mall and bought new clothes, but after shopping we didn't return to my dad's. Instead we got on Interstate 91 and headed toward Vermont. I was a little confused, and when I questioned Bill about where we were going he explained that he was doing what my mother wanted: keeping her kids together.

We arrived at a little chalet in Vermont late that night. Bill called my dad and told him that if everyone agreed to let James and me go back to New Hampshire with him, we would come back for Mom's funeral. Otherwise, he would make sure we were never seen or heard from again. He was a very persuasive man who always got what he wanted. Dad knew that Bill was powerful and influential enough to make sure that happened. Once my dad agreed Bill brought us back to Massachusetts to attend Mom's services.

James and I were brought in for a private viewing. (Jason did not attend.) It had been four days since being told of our mother's death, but over a week since I'd last seen her, waving as she headed to her car after dropping us off at Dad's. *She promised she'd be back to get us.* My heart began to pound as we entered the funeral home where the viewing would take place. The stale smell and frigid temperature of the room were frightening. Fear gripped me. I wasn't sure what to do.

Out of the corner of my eye I could see the casket. It was surrounded by flowers and a huge wreath with a ribbon that said "Mother; daughter; friend." My heart pounded faster with every step. I could see the profile of her face as I inched my way closer until I was looking down at her. She didn't even look like my mom. She was wearing a white silk top with a high collar and bow around the neck (something my mother would have never worn), a red suit jacket and black pants. With the makeup she had on, she looked more like a mannequin than a person. She looked like she was sleeping. I couldn't understand why I could physically see her but she couldn't wake up. I reached in and touched her hand. It was cold and hard. As I silently begged her to open her eyes, my head screamed, *Wake up, Mommy. Please wake up.*

At that moment I realized that my mom would never again tuck me into bed at night. Her long, beautiful hair would never again fall in my face tickling my nose as she bent down to kiss my forehead. I would never hear her call my name or listen to her familiar laugh, the one that filled me with so much love and warmth. I was saying good-bye to her, and once I walked out of this room I would never see her again. I'd have only my memories, ones I prayed would never fade.

After our private viewing there were "calling hours" for everyone else. I couldn't believe how many people there were, each one looking at me with pity but not offering any words of comfort. When we all went back to my grandparents' house, my brothers and I were put in one of the back bedrooms, isolated from all the grieving friends and family. The solid gold locket containing a piece of Mom's hair that we were each given didn't take away the emptiness and fear I was feeling. We listened to friends and family out in the living room sharing laughter and tears. No one came in to see us. There were no condolences, no answers to our mounting questions. We grieved alone, just the three of us.

The next day, March 3, 1981, was cold and blustery, typical for that time of year and very fitting for a funeral. Bill, my dad, my mom's two best friends Linda and Nard, my two brothers and I sat in the limo heading to the cemetery to bury my mother. In the limo behind us were my grandparents, my Uncle Skippy and cousin JoJo, Auntie Mary, Uncle Fred, and cousins Jessica and Justin. As we approached the gravesite, I saw hundreds of people gathered. It was the biggest funeral Wakefield had ever seen. There were so many flowers you could hardly see the casket.

I leaned over to Nard and said, "When you hear about things like this, you think it can only happen to other people." Sadly, I'd come to the stark realization that terrible things could happen to anyone at anytime.

Nard reached over and took my hand, giving it a tight squeeze and then turned her face away.

Standing at the gravesite I stared at the casket in front of me as I listened intently to the priest. He spoke about heaven and what a beautiful place it was. He talked about the angels and how my mother was with them now, looking down on us. He spoke of the legacy Mom had left her three children, the wonderful memories we all had and how we should share them in order to keep her spirit alive. He explained that life is a precious gift and when our earthly bodies die our eternal bodies are born. He said that we will see my mom again someday when we get to heaven. But this only confused me more. I knew that Mom's friends had put various items up her sleeve the night before. I had heard them joking and laughing about how they could continue the party up in heaven. It hadn't fazed me at the time but in contrast to what the priest was saying I had so many more questions and no one to ask. Everyone was so stricken by their own grief that they couldn't see my brothers and me, or our needs.

As they lowered my mother into the freshly dug ground, I looked over at James. Without even speaking, I knew what he was thinking. Like me, he wanted to open that casket and scream for her to wake up. Our eyes locked and at that moment I knew our bond was sealed, that from then on, all we had was each other.

Later that night, after the funeral, we returned to New Hampshire with Bill. It was rather fitting to move somewhere else given that our world had drastically changed. On the way he told us that we would never have to go back to the farm again. He said that we would live with Uncle Al while a new house was being built. Al adored my mother and had always been there to protect her when Bill was away on "business." The anguish Al felt over Mom's death was all over his face. When we arrived at his house late that night he couldn't even look us in the eye.

My brothers and I went straight to bed. But I couldn't sleep. I heard Al tell Bill that Suds had disappeared and there was an all-points-bulletin out for his arrest.

"He'd better hope the cops find him before I do," I heard Bill say.

I listened as they talked for a little while longer and then Bill retreated to the bedroom next door. The image of my mother lying in her coffin haunted me but the sound of Bill having sex with Al's sister, Betty, in the next room on the very night we buried my mom made me sick.

Chapter Seven

Bill's promise of never having to go back to the farm was like so many promises made to us then. Within a few months we were living there again, along with Bill's new girlfriend Betty. There were many changes from the last time I had been there right before my mom died. The spiral staircase had been removed and was replaced with a custom wooden one. All along the railing were wood-burnings of wildlife. The living room and the walls leading to the basement had a fresh coat of paint and there was all new furniture. When I asked Bill what had happened to everything all he said was, "I thought we needed a change."

As independent as Bill was, he was severely co-dependent when it came to women. I think he was also probably worried about having someone to take care of us. After all, he was gone three or four days every week on "business." Betty was Uncle Al's sister, a young, naïve twenty-two-year-old single mother. She was enamored with Bill and did her best to be good to the three of us newly orphaned children. For a time I felt special. Betty was especially devoted to me. Maybe she just felt sorry for me.

A couple of months before Mom died, she'd enrolled James and me in "The Royal Eagles," an organized Drum and Drill Corp. comprised of fifty kids from six towns in the local area. Mom had wanted us to learn discipline and dedication and be around other kids our age. I came to admire the folks who were committed to helping us continue our participation in the Corp. If it weren't for the insistence of the other parents and the help of our neighbors who drove us, James and I probably wouldn't have continued with the Royal Eagles. Thank God for them! They made sure we stayed with the organization, telling Bill, "It's what Patty would have wanted for her kids." I will be forever grateful to them.

Royal Eagles met twice a week for practice and marched in every county fair in the tri-state area; New Hampshire, Maine and Vermont. We were each assigned a number (mine was seventeen) and a position. I carried a rifle and a flag while James played the snare drum. Our military-style uniforms signified our rank. I started out as a Private and graduated six years later as a Captain. I attribute much of what I learned about commitment, acceptance and loyalty to this time spent with the Royal Eagles. Through this experience I gained self confidence, friendships and recognition. It showed me how to be a person of quality—quite a contrast to what I was being taught at the farm.

In January 1982, almost a year after my mother's death, Suds stood trial for her murder. He had actually been found in Pennsylvania a week after her death and was extradited to New Hampshire. Now he faced first degree murder charges.

With the trial going on, things were pretty stressful around the farm. Bill was on edge because of the friends who were being called as witnesses and the questions they were being asked. People from past and present would stop by the farm on a daily basis during the trial. I thought it was to show their support or to offer comfort to my brothers and me, but it was actually to apologize to Bill for what they had divulged under oath. "I'm sorry, man, I had to tell the truth," was the perpetual introduction as they entered the living room shaking their heads in disbelief at what their lives had become.

The only person from Mom's family who came to the trial was my Auntie. I guess it was too much for my grandparents to take, but I never understood why they never even came by to see my brothers and me during such a trying time. Despite all the information divulged during the trial about the goings-on at the farm, no one tried to remove us from that environment. Social Services came by once or twice, but the focus was never about the well-being of us kids.

One day about a week into the trial, James and I had to go to court and testify. It was a frigid day and the long drive down Route 25 to the courthouse in Haverhill seemed endless. There wasn't much to look at except fields and an isolated house here and there. We called it "cow country." Once in a while we'd pass through a small farming town. For the most part, the thirty-five minute ride was silent. Bill and Uncle Al sat up front in Bill's new black Ford extended cab truck while James and I sat in the back.

When we pulled into the parking lot, the huge brick building seemed out of place in such a desolate area. The sign said "Grafton County Courthouse." Having been raised to distrust police, I was very nervous seeing all the cops in uniform. Bill led us up the stairs and to the courtroom where the trial had been taking place. People started filling the room. Nard and Linda were already sitting down behind prosecutor Paul Roudes and his associates. In front of him was a large table displaying various items from the farm used as evidence during the trial. Next to the table was a large poster with a schematic layout of the inside of the house.

As we settled in our seats next to Nard and Linda, a side door to my right opened and *he* came in—the one responsible for everyone being there that day, the one responsible for changing my life forever. The police officers on either side of Suds led him toward the defense table. With hands and feet shackled, he shuffled in with his head lowered and his greasy hair hanging in his eyes. Wearing a green-and-white striped shirt and dungarees, he looked up at me. When our eyes met, he brought his hands up to his neck and made a gesture of slicing his throat. With that, officers and bailiffs scurried over to us and escorted me out.

"I'm sorry, miss. You'll have to wait out here," was the only explanation I got.

I was left, alone, on a wooden bench outside the courtroom. Curious, I eventually made my way to the double brown doors and tried to listen to what was going on. But an officer came over to me and gently moved me away. A few minutes later, two sheriffs brought me into the control room and showed me all the cameras and TV screens that monitored the building. At the time I figured they thought I'd be interested in seeing the neat stuff they used to watch criminals in the courtroom. Looking back now, I realize they probably thought, *This poor little girl's mother was murdered. We should distract her and keep her busy while the trial goes on downstairs.* When the nice men brought me back to the benches outside the courtroom, one of them handed me a book to help pass the time. It was called *The Diary of Ann Frank*. I sat for the next few hours reading and waiting for the day to be over.

Since my mom's death my brother James was the only person I could talk to about her, but during the trial something happened to him and after that he would literally put his hand up and say, "Stop! Don't talk about it." James had to testify because he was the last person to speak to Mom before she died and had heard Suds in the background. Nard later explained to me that as James walked toward the stand, he passed the evidence table. The broken butcher knife was Exhibit A. Beside the knife were the clothes that my mother was wearing at the time of her death, still covered with dry blood. A huge board on an easel displayed blueprints of the layout of the farm with a body drawn at the bottom of the staircase. Horrified and shocked by what he saw lying on the long wooden table, what little life remained in him was drained. The recognizable fire poker and large photos of the crime scene were undoubtedly the most damaging to his already fragile psyche.

The last thing I recall about the trial was Bill announcing a few weeks later that after a short deliberation, the jury had found Suds guilty and sentenced him to life without parole. After that, the trial was never mentioned again. For the most part neither was my mother.

Mom had always been interested in spirituality, reincarnation and the afterlife. One night, shortly after the trial ended I fell asleep in the master bedroom. I suddenly awoke, sat up and looked toward the stairs. My mom was standing at the top. The room was black but a light surrounded her naked silhouette. With her hands on the handrails, she looked over at me and, with a self-satisfied smile, descended the stairs as the light faded with her image. Everyone I told said I was dreaming, but I knew better. I truly believe my mother's presence was there that day and every day afterwards watching over me.

The only person who believed my dream was Nard because she had had her own experience with my mom's presence. It happened a few days after her death. Nard and Linda had been at the house getting ready to pack up Mom's belongings. They were talking about how much they missed her when Nard said she could feel my mom's presence and the scent of her perfume. Suddenly, a basket abruptly fell from a beam in the kitchen. No one else was at the farm that day. Nard believed it was Mom's way of telling them she was there. Right after that, a stray cat showed up out of nowhere. It was very odd. The cat would sit on the kitchen counter and watch us all eat dinner at night. She stayed for a while, had a litter of kittens and then, as quick as she had come, disappeared. I believe it was my mom coming to make sure we were all okay.

After her death I chose to move my bedroom into the cellar, the very place her body was found. I felt close to her down there. I swear I could feel her hug me at night and sometimes even smell the perfume she used to wear.

Having clearly bitten off more than she could chew, Betty eventually suffered the fallout of being Bill's woman. It soon became too much and she succumbed to the nasty addiction of cocaine and sweet little Betty became known as "the coke whore." About a year after my mom's trial was over, I had just turned twelve, Betty showed me a secret hiding spot in the closet of the master bedroom. Removing a floorboard underneath the carpet, she pulled out a freezer bag full of cocaine. After shoveling a few spoonfuls into a tiny vial, she offered me some, I assume to keep me quiet. I politely declined and left the room. If Bill knew, he would have been livid but I kept it to myself. That was when I learned that knowledge was power. The more I had on Betty the more it benefited me and I could use against her when the time was right.

Still, Betty was young and foolish enough to believe that she was the only woman in Bill's life. Even at my young age I knew better. I will never forget the day she dragged me into the bathroom, pulled down her panties and sat on the floor. She spread herself open, showing me her nasty herpes and said, "Look what Billy did to me."

Mortified, all I could say was, "I'm sorry."

After that I knew this chick needed to go and it was up to me to make sure that happened. I had known for a while that Betty was screwing around with some of Bills friends for drugs. I took it upon myself to call the wife of one of them and told her. The wife then told Bill who confronted Betty. It caused a big scene, and a huge fight ensued between Bill and Betty. The final straw (no pun intended) was when I caught her stealing our social security checks. Bill kicked her ass out as fast as he'd moved her in.

The day she left was almost as traumatic as the day we found out our mother had died. By then Jason was almost five and Betty had been his "mother figure" for the last two years. Too young to understand the reason why she was leaving he wrapped his little arms and legs around her leg, crying and begging her not to leave. James and I were standing on the porch watching as Betty looked down at Jason, kicked him off her and walked down the steps and out of our lives forever. My heart broke for my little brother but I was glad she was gone and swore I wouldn't let Bill move any more women into the house. You might think this was where the horror ended, but it was just the beginning...

Chapter Eight

The vestiges of my childhood died with my mom. The only person who stayed working on the farm after her murder was Uncle Al. Everyone else just drifted apart or moved away. Even though she was rarely, if ever, mentioned just having those who knew Mom around, reminded me of her. No one seemed to realize that my brothers and I still needed the familiarity of being surrounded by the friends and family who knew and loved her in order to keep her spirit alive. When we visited Nana and Pa in Massachusetts, they never talked about her or asked us how we were doing. Pictures were slowly put away. It was as if she had never existed.

On the rare occasion I saw my dad—when we stopped by the Italian American Club—he would always be drunk. He was a perfect example of someone who abused alcohol to ease the pain of all his failures in life. After my mom's death he seemed to fall deeper and deeper into the darkness of his alcoholism. My dad would invariably be found sitting on the same stool at the end of the bar with a beer in his hand. I guess if my dad taught me anything it was how *not* to be. Alcohol never interested me, but I was curious about the fascination everyone had with marijuana. I wanted to know why everyone at the farm seemed to smoke it every day, all day.

The first time I actually tried pot was during my mom's trial. I was eleven years old at the time. One night after eating dinner at The Steak Barn with Bill, Uncle Al brought James and me home to the farm. Driving up the dark dirt road at around seven-thirty at night in Al's Volkswagen Van, he took a joint from the visor and lit it up.

"Why do you smoke that?" I asked.

"It helps me relax," he said as he took a long drag.

"What does it make you feel like?" I pried a little further.

"Do you want to try it, Jenny?" he asked. "If you're that curious I'll let you try a little. But you have to promise not to tell anybody."

"I promise," I responded, excited to finally see what all the hype was about.

"Just inhale a little bit. You don't want to take too much," Uncle Al warned.

My eyes crossed as I brought the half-smoked joint to my lips, watching the red fiery end the whole time. It got brighter as I took a drag. It burned my throat and I started to cough.

"Here, James. You want to try?" I asked, still trying to get my breath.

Following my lead he too took a small drag and then handed it back to Uncle Al. Within minutes my body began to tingle and then felt like it went numb. For a while I was scared. By the time we pulled into the driveway, I was sure that anyone who saw me would know I was high.

The farm was never without people around, so as we got out of the van Uncle Al said, "You kids might want to go on up to your rooms for a while and watch television."

Bill was out on a date with Carry, the waitress from The Steak Barn, so James and I went up to the master bedroom and watched "Fantasy Island." We laughed hysterically at things that probably weren't funny to anyone else, but the giggles were something we couldn't seem to control. Uncle Al came up to check on us a couple of times. I asked him when the funny feeling would go away and why my mouth felt so dry.

"I thought you kids might be hungry," he said as he entered the bedroom with a bowl of popcorn and two cans of soda.

"Thanks," we said in unison.

Even though I didn't really like how it made me feel that first time. I continued to smoke marijuana almost every day after that. I don't know why exactly; maybe it was to feel like I fit in with everyone else. Eventually it became my coping mechanism.

Bill didn't know James and I knew where he kept his supply. At any given time the two-story barn was filled with more than just hay for the animals. We knew that the bails wrapped in green plastic were not to be touched. But James and I would grab a zip-lock baggie and take a few handfuls from the bail that always had a fist-sized hole in it. Then we'd go into the bathroom and roll a joint, flushing the rest down the toilet so we wouldn't get caught. Most of the time there was enough for at least another three joints, but it didn't matter; we knew where to get more. Then we would drive our four-wheelers into the woods. One of us would act as the lookout while the other took a few drags.

With Betty gone and Bill needing to take a "business trip," someone had to be around the farm to watch us kids. He asked one of the girls from the Hells Angels named, of all things, Patti. She came up and babysat my brothers and me for a few days and brought a friend named Tiger with her. Tiger was an artist and painted the most amazing mural on my bedroom wall. It was life-sized characters of the entire Charlie Brown Gang walking around my room.

I have always said that normal is what you know, however, I don't think it was all that normal for my brother and I to be sitting in a hot tub filled with Mr. Bubbles and two chicks from the Hells Angels drinking expensive champagne and smoking a joint soaked in hash oil (a more potent form of marijuana) at the age of twelve. But that was another thing we did with Patti and Tiger that weekend.

Bill wasn't very happy when he got home and found out what we'd done. It's the only time I ever recall him referring to my mom. "Your mother would kick my ass if she were alive." I think that's when he realized he needed a woman around full time to take care of things while he was away.

I vividly recall the day that happened. Coincidently, three girls had come up to the farm on the same day to see Bill, all vying to move in. Each one had something going on with Bill, either past or present. Carry, the waitress from the Steak Barn, who Bill had been seeing on and off for a few years (including when my mom was still alive), was one of the girls there that day. She had been in love with Bill since she was in high school and had been spending a lot of time with him.

Barbara, a chick who Bill fooled around with a couple of times, had stopped by in her red Jeep Wrangler to see him. Barbara liked Bill much more than he liked her and wanted nothing more than to be his girlfriend and move onto the farm. Last was pathetic little Betty, who wanted to move back. *Over my dead body*, I thought. I didn't even acknowledge that she was there, even when I saw her sucking up to my little brothers, making all nice and everything.

What a sight it was that day! The cat-fighting was almost humorous. It was as if they were applying for a job or something.

Bill came up to James and me and said, "Hey, kids, we're going for a ride."

We jumped in the back of Barbara's Jeep and, with Carry in the front passenger seat, drove up to "the property," past the Christmas Tree Orchard, through Thai Land and down to Pelican Point where Bill pulled off and stopped the car.

Turning around, Bill said, "We need to talk to you kids. Somebody needs to be in the house when I'm not around. Carry has known me for a very long time and she wants to be the one to move in."

James and I looked at each other and, as usual, knew what the other was thinking. I spoke up and said, "You know what, Carry? You seem like a very nice person but Bill does things to women and we don't want to see that happen to you."

"Billy and I have known each other for a long time, and that won't happen to me," she said, so self-assured.

James and I knew it didn't matter what we thought; what would happen would happen. And with that, we just shrugged our shoulders and said, "Okay."

Carry was bubbly and nice, always happy and smiling, when she first moved in. Her physique was similar to my mother's but her long hair was black. She tried hard to be a good stepmother to us. Even though she was nice to me in the beginning, I don't think she really liked me because she thought I was Bill's favorite, not to mention that I looked a lot like my mom. I don't think she warmed up to Jason very much because he represented Mom and Bill. James was her favorite, probably, because he was so quiet and never spoke up. James did what he was told, without arguing or talking back.

Right before Carry moved onto the farm Bill had brought the "Vermont people" back in to clear and till a portion of the 100-acre lot he had purchased up the road from the farm when Mom was still alive. We called it "the plantation."

The Vermont people were just a few of the friends and freaks that hung around the farm. These were the same people my mom had used as an example of being tolerant of others. But, the older I got the creepier they seemed. Gopher was the guy who brought in all the heavy equipment when Bill was originally building the farm, and again when he cleared "the plantation." Gopher was around twenty years old. He was your typical-nasty-little-johndeer-hat-wearing-flannelshirt-with-dirty-levi-sporting-a-red-scruffy-beard, kind of guy. He gave me the heebie-jeebies. He had a thirteen-year-old girlfriend named Jasmine who would come up to the farm with him and hit on every guy there, including my little brother James. One day I went down to my bedroom in the basement. When I flicked on the light, Gopher and his girlfriend were having sex.

"Oops," I said, startled at the sight.

"No, that's okay. Join us," they invited.

"Uh, no thanks," I replied, horrified, as I shut off the light and scurried away.

Over the course of the next few years, Bill went through many phases. He would get an idea in his head and then hire people, usually James and me, to do all the work. Our pay was "room and board."

We already had the vegetable gardens and James and I would spend hours in the hot blazing sun weeding and watering all five acres. The first phase Bill got into after that was the fruit phase. He would load James and I in his pickup truck early in the morning with the hemp-weaved baskets he'd brought back from one of his "trips" to the islands. Carry would pack us sandwiches and drinks in a green cooler. Bill would dump us off in the orchard to pick hundreds of bushels of blueberries and strawberries until he picked us up later in the day. This chore didn't replace our weeding and watering of the vegetable gardens; it was *added* to our list of responsibilities around the farm.

After that, Bill bought a wood chipper and rented it out. He also rented out James' and my services. On weekends Bill would load us into the truck that pulled the chipper and take us to the houses of the customers with whom he'd set up jobs. Bill would stay long enough to show us what needed to be cut down and then leave us with the wood chipper and detailed instructions, sometimes for up to six hours. It's truly amazing that we never cut off any body parts!

Then there was the pheasant phase. He bought between five and eight hundred birds, but before we could slaughter them they escaped. Bill wasn't very happy about all the money he lost in that deal. He stood to make quite a profit in the resale; but I heard pheasant season was very good for hunters in the Wentworth area that year.

When Bill decided to add Christmas trees, instead of a party, I spent my fourteenth birthday planting over five-thousand trees. That was also the summer Bill decided to have a fruit and vegetable stand out on Tenney

Mountain Highway. When I wasn't working in the gardens and orchard, Bill would drop me off at eight o'clock in the morning and come back and pick me up at six. I spent that summer standing in ninety-degree heat selling all the produce James and I had spent hours picking and harvesting. The only good thing that came out of that summer was meeting Philip, a seventeen-year- old senior in high school. He was my first boyfriend—my first everything – and we dated for about a year.

Bill rewarded us the only way he knew how. I remember the first time he handed me a joint and didn't expect me to pass it along, as he had always done before. By then I had already been smoking for a couple of years, unbeknownst to Bill who was only aware of the one time in the hot tub. But this time I could tell he wanted me to take a hit, so I did and then passed it to the next person. Bill never said a word but from then on, James and I were invited to sit in on the after-dinner family tradition. Only now, I cleaned the dinner dishes while Bill would sit in front of the TV and twist up a fatty. After that, James and I got a bag of pot tied with a nice red bow in our Christmas stockings every year.

As far back as I can remember my brothers and I had been conditioned to lie about Bill's "business." One night around ten o'clock, James and I were relaxing on the couch and Bill came busting through the front door, cursing. Startled, we sat up, unsure if it was something we had done.

"God-damn f****** idiots can't do anything right! Get your shoes on. I need your help down the road," he snapped at us.

Scrambling out the door behind him, James and I didn't have a clue what was going on. We followed Bill down the dark dirt road, flashlights in hand. As we got closer to all the excitement, we saw a tractor-trailer jackknifed in the road. Two police cruisers were on the back side of the eighteen-wheeler. Approaching the cops, we heard them suggest to the driver that he unload the truck.

"Why don't you empty the contents out of the back to make the truck lighter and easier to upright," they suggested and even offered to help.

Panicked, Bill said, "That's not necessary. If we get enough manpower on the other side we can turn it back onto its wheels."

"What's in the back?" one of the officers asked curiously as he walked around, shining his flashlight.

"Peat moss," Bill answered before turning his attention to the driver and yelling, "Hey, F***head, unhook the trailer from the cab!"

Visibly scared out of his mind, the driver released the trailer and took a position to help right the situation. Five strong men, two state troopers and two kids managed to get the trailer back on its wheels. Soon it was hooked back up and on its way to the farm. Relieved, Bill shook the officers' hands, thanked them for their help and turned to walk back to the farm. As soon as we were out of earshot he said under his breath, "Suckers."

While walking back to the farm, I recalled the last time we had been in a similar situation. I was seven and we still lived in Wakefield. It was the middle of the night and we were driving home in Bill's pickup truck. James and I were sleeping in the back. I awoke to a light shining in my face through the side window. We had been pulled over on the Interstate.

"What's in the trash bags?" the cop had asked Bill as he walked around the truck, investigating every inch.

"It's dirty laundry," Bill had explained. "We're on our way home from camping up north."

Accepting his explanation, the officer had let Bill go with a warning to slow down. "Have a good night, folks," he'd said as he headed back to his cruiser.

When we got home I found out that the four thirty-gallon bags of "dirty laundry" actually contained marijuana.

As I predicted it wasn't long before Carry fell under Bill's strange spell and after awhile couldn't fake being nice anymore. It seemed to me that all women who became involved with Bill (including my mom) thought they could change him—the rebellious soul who was always looking for his next adventure. Each one thought she could tame his wild heart, only to be left shattered and confused by his games. Bill had a way of making you think you were crazy, and after awhile you started questioning your own sanity. I've seen it happen time and time again, even with me. A conversation would start off one way and always take a dramatic turn, leaving me wondering what I was even talking about.

Overwhelmed by all the responsibilities Carry quickly turned into a hypochondriac and started hibernating upstairs in the master bedroom. She always complained about everything she had to do to keep the farm running while Bill was away on "business". In reality all she had to do was boss me and James around and make us do everything. We were no longer mere residents of the farm; we were slaves on it.

Chapter Nine

In September of 1983, Bill had decided he wanted to be a turkey farmer; hence the name "Bill's Turkey Farm" was born. He enlisted the help of friends from Massachusetts whose family had owned a turkey farm for over fifty years. Tony and his wife Sue moved to New Hampshire and lived in the little "staff" house. A meat room (we called it the "kill room") was built out back next to two large turkey pens. We got the turkeys when they were only hours old and still needed to be under heating lamps. Someone had to be with them at all times and Tony was that someone. The turkeys were like newborns to Tony, and he knew everything there was to know about taking care of them.

Once the turkeys were old enough to be outside, they were put in an 80 x 100-foot pen. James and I had the responsibility of changing the shavings in the pen and watering and feeding the turkeys every day. The turkeys also needed to be inoculated against disease, another one of our jobs. James would catch them while I injected them with 1cc of antibiotic. A syringe could inoculate ten birds, so ensuring I didn't give them too much was a difficult task—especially with all the flapping and scratching they did, which hurt like hell. (In all the chaos throughout the years, I'm sure I must have inoculated myself and James a few times. As a result, we probably have damn good immune systems!) The actual killing process didn't begin until November, so while Tony and Sue set everything up in the processing plant, which contained the newest, most high-tech equipment Bill could buy James and I continued to do our other chores around the farm.

Two weeks before Thanksgiving, the actual killing process began. Tony, Sue, James and I would get up early in the morning and head up to the kill room around seven o'clock. Tony would decide how many turkeys we would kill that day, usually around five hundred. Right outside the kill room was a makeshift pen. I have to say that turkeys are really stupid animals—they would walk right to their death.

The whole process had to be done in one day, start to finish. This required us to wear rubber clothes; suspender pants, jackets labeled "evisceration team" with our name underneath, rubber boots, gloves and hat. Tony was the executioner and did the actual killing. He would hang three turkeys at a time by their feet and tap them on the head with a stun gun, rendering them unconscious. Then he would go back and slice their throats, leaving them to bleed while he went and got three more birds. If a turkey wasn't knocked out enough, it would start flapping its wings and that became a bloody mess.

Once the turkeys were finished bleeding, Tony would come back and cut their feet off and put them into the "scalder," which rotated them in hot water, loosening the feathers. A rack kept them in the water, and when the turkeys came out they were extremely hot. Afterwards, the turkeys were brought to the "cyclone," a huge metal contraption with millions of tiny rubber fingers that plucked the feathers off the turkeys as they spun around. This thing spun extremely fast and was very loud. When the cyclone spit the turkeys out a little door, they'd land in a stainless steel laundry cart on wheels. James and I would be there to grab them and hang them on another rack, pulling off any remaining feathers with pliers and chopping their heads off using a huge hedge clipper. After that, the turkeys were placed in a 500-gallon stainless steel tank filled with cold water to cool.

We continued this until all the turkeys selected to be processed that day were killed. The floors were concrete with several drains located throughout the building. Rubber boots were a necessity, as the floor would become flooded with blood. Every so often we would have to hose it down because the blood would coagulate and become very sticky.

At that point, it would be around noon and we'd take a break. We'd go down to the farm, get some lunch, smoke some dope and hang out for and hour or so before going back up for the next phase. Bill always had lunch waiting for us. One minute he'd be riding around the farm (it was so big it took a four-wheeler or golf cart to get around) verbally assaulting us, and the next minute he'd be saying, "Hey, you want something to eat? You must be starving." He would make up an enormous lunch, not just sandwiches. We'd usually have pasta or stew, something hot and hearty to carry us through. Usually I had to do dishes after every meal, but not during "kill season."

After putting our rubber clothes back on, we'd begin the long tedious process of eviscerating the turkeys. All four of us would stand around a ten-foot-long table, pull the guts and organs out of the turkeys and put them together as giblets. We'd start by cutting this small skin tag off the turkey's backside. Then we'd flip the bird over and cut along the back of its neck, pulling back the skin using all four fingers. We were very careful not to rupture the "sack," a membrane full of turkey food. Then we'd turn the bird over on its back again, slice a hole from its neck to its butt and cut the rest of the butt off, leaving the opening to the body cavity. At that point the work became very delicate, as we'd gently coax each organ out. Usually everything came out whole, but just in case it didn't, we'd insert a heavy-duty water pick with teeth on the end and rinse out the cavity, scrapping any remaining pieces.

This process usually took four or five hours. During this time, James and I had some of our best conversations and, on occasion, gross-out contests.

"I dare you to bite into the heart of that turkey," James challenged me once. I didn't even hesitate as I picked up the heart and bit down. Blood squirted everywhere and James declared, "You're the winner." After a brief pause he followed by, "That was really gross, Jen."

It was usually around 5:00 PM when we'd finish the evisceration process We would take another break, head down to the main house, eat some food, smoke some more dope and then go back up for the final packaging phase, which took about three hours.

The turkeys were hung twelve at a time on the rack so we could put the giblets inside. Then the turkeys were weighed, bagged and stored in a huge, 15 x 25-foot walk-in freezer according to their weight. Thirteen hours and 500 turkeys later, we were done for the day.

We did this every year for the next six years. The "kill season" took about two weeks and Bill would take James and me out of school for those weeks every November.

Tony and Sue became the closest people to me during those couple of years they lived on the farm. Sue was my best friend and the only positive role model I had. Despite the fact that they smoked weed with my brother and me, I credit them for many positive things, one being my deep appreciation for nature and where I live. We would often take rides in the car and look at some of New Hampshire's breathtaking views. The "Old Man on the Mountain" was one of our favorites. In the winter they would take us skiing at Cannon Mountain and Killington. It was great doing the "normal" things that most kids do.

Being around nothing but boys all the time, I acted more like a tomboy. Sue was the one who taught me how to be girly. I talked to her about girl things, like boys. Since I was dating Philip, a senior, when I was a freshman, I attended his prom in the spring of 1985. Sue was the one who took me shopping for a dress. It was during that shopping trip that she said to me, "Don't grow up any faster than you already have, Jen." She knew what I'd been exposed to at the farm.

"You should wait before having sex. Respect your body, because if you don't no one else will," she said with the utmost sincerity.

I didn't have the heart to tell her it was already too late. My first time had been the previous summer, with Philip, behind the bleachers at the Plymouth Fair when I was fourteen.

By this time, Carry was totally stressed out. Everything was traumatic; she was bitter and nasty. She was no longer that lively, smiling person who'd moved into the farm and told us that things would be different. She'd started out being really nice and kind, asking how our day was and driving us where we needed to go. But now everything was an imposition and we had to walk on eggshells around her all the time. One day the bus broke down and we were about two miles from the farm. We called her from one of the little farm houses and asked her to come and get us because it was cold and snowing.

"I don't have time to do that," she said and hung up the phone.

As it was, we had to walk down the hill every morning about three quarters of a mile to catch the bus and back up the hill in the afternoon to get home. A few times in bad weather the bus driver would take us all the way home because we were the last drop, but that didn't happen very often.

Only once since Bill started the turkey business did I see Carry ever come up to the kill room to help. It was during the packaging process, but she was more in the way than anything because we had our own system. She wasn't up there for more than an hour and by the time we were done for the night she did nothing but complain about how much her body ached from all the work she'd done in the kill room. Later, I overheard her bitching to a friend on the phone about the stress of having to take care of the farm and the house and us kids. She told her friend that she'd had a miscarriage a few months earlier because of all the strain I put on her. Even though I couldn't stand Carry I felt guilty that I'd caused her to have a miscarriage and that I was the reason she was so miserable, so from that point on I pretty much took over all the responsibilities of the house.

But this just made me hate her more. I couldn't understand how she could blame me for so much. I was only fifteen years old and I was already doing all the dishes and had a huge workload in the house as well as on the farm, not to mention my schoolwork. It got to the point where I couldn't even fake being nice to her anymore. I despised her more and more every day.

In the fall of that same year, 1985, Tony and Sue left the farm and moved back to Massachusetts. Before they left, Tony and Bill had an argument over money. Tony had taken some of his equipment that he'd loaned Bill when he first started the turkey business. The argument escalated and to frighten Tony, Bill brandished a Smith and Wesson 9mm semi-automatic pistol and fired a shot. Troopers were called to defuse the situation. Unaware that Bill was a felon from an incident in Massachusetts in 1976 when he was a teenager, they gave him a receipt for the return of his gun. (This situation would later come back to bite Bill in the ass.)

Being November, the start of another "kill season", Bill put Uncle Skippy (my mom's brother) in Tony's position. Now the evisceration team was made up of James and me, Uncle Skippy and our thirteen year old cousin JoJo.

Chapter Ten

The first time I really began to feel like an adult was the summer before Paul and Sue left. It was during one of Bill's three-day parties. I had just turned fifteen years old and had recently developed boobs (I was a late bloomer). It was also the first and only time I tried cocaine.

Everything Bill did was over-the-top, and his annual three-day party was no exception. Every year he threw a big shindig for about a hundred and fifty of his closest friends. For a week before the party the farm was bustling with crews getting things ready. Huts were built for food and shelter. A makeshift bar was made from plywood and sawhorses (complete with bartender). Generators were brought in for electricity and port-a-potties were set up. A trailer used to haul missiles was brought in so the three bands that rotated sets throughout the weekend could have a platform on which to set up.

When Bill threw a party he didn't throw just any party. He didn't get just a couple cases of beer; he got a couple hundred cases of every kind of beer. And he didn't get just one bottle of alcohol; he got a couple bottles of every kind of hard alcohol and kegs of soda, complete with taps. The grill was stocked with hamburgers, hotdogs, chicken, steak and sausage. Official tickets for this three-day extravaganza were sold in advance—$25 including food or $10.00 for just drinks. T-shirts were made up—tank tops for the women and regular shirts for the guys. They were black with his slogan "Bill's Turkey Farm - Let Us Put Our Breasts in Your Mouth."

Jumping on my dirt bike on that hot July day, I led the white delivery trucks up the road about three quarters of a mile to "the property" where the annual party would be held. When I reached the top, I stopped to take in the breathtaking view of the mountains and let the trucks catch up. Turning onto Pelican Point, I sped down the dirt road to a clearing in front of the lake where it would all take place. In just hours, it would be a sea of people. That year Bill added free helicopter rides to his list of attractions. As James and I rode around showing caterers where to set up and delivery trucks where to go, people started to file in. By nightfall, campers, trucks and tents lined the road and the party was well under way.

    I bopped around, visiting old friends and making new ones. Every campsite seemed to have something different to offer. I would hang out for a while, smoke some dope, chat for a bit and then move on. The people at one campsite I visited were doing cocaine. I indulged and did "a line," acting like I'd done it before, and then moved on. As I left their camper, I ran into a friend—actually, it was my ex-boyfriend Philip's best friend. Thankful that I was around someone I knew and trusted, I told him I had just done a "rail" and didn't like how it was making me feel.

    "Let's go take a helicopter ride. The scenery will be breathtaking," he suggested, clearly high himself.

    I sat up front with the pilot, and for forty-five minutes we flew high above the White Mountains and lakes. It was the most amazing experience of my life. The aerial view of the farm made me really appreciate what we had. Despite all the hard work, I had to admit it was a beautiful piece of property.

    When we got back on the ground, things had begun to get intense at the party. David and Tina, a "Vermont" couple, were fighting and David was holding Tina hostage in their camper at gunpoint. It took Bill a few hours to calm David down and get the gun away from him. David and Tina owned a Mexican shop in Vermont where they sold things like blankets and other décor. Years earlier, while in Mexico buying supplies, Tina had gotten mixed up in a baby smuggling operation and spent some time in a Mexican prison. (A few years after this incident at the three-day party, I found out that David was in an automobile accident and killed someone. He couldn't handle the guilt and a few months later called up Tina, and while she was on the phone with him, blew himself away.)

Gopher and Jasmine were at this party and again propositioned me to join them in an orgy. They came up to me and told me how beautiful I was.

"Yeah, I don't think so," I responded in disgust. "Man, Bill's got some freaky friends," I mumbled to myself as I walked away.

Then I ran into George the Greek, one of Bill's friends whom I hadn't seen in a while. A member of the Hells Angels, he was a beautiful, Greek Adonis-looking man, about six foot three with pumped-up muscles and a glass eye. He owned a Gold's Gym in Massachusetts.

Sliding an arm around my waist, he came up and gave me a big hug.

"My, how grown up you've become, my little Jenny," he said flirtatiously.

"Hey George, It's great to see you," I said with a big smile and a bigger hug.

"What a beautiful young lady you have turned into," he continued.

As we walked toward the food hut, I asked him if Tiger was with him. "She did an amazing painting on my bedroom wall a few years ago," I told him.

"Oh, God no," George said matter-of-factly. "She died of AIDS last year."

"Sorry to hear that," I replied without emotion. Stuff like that no longer shocked me.

"Well, what can you expect from a prostitute?" He shrugged. "I'll catch up with you later, baby," he said quickly, obviously seeing someone else he wanted to talk to.

Seeing George that night had reminded me of an incident that had taken place earlier that summer with his dog. He had a pit-bull named Angel that would only listen to certain people. Bill was one of them, which did a lot for his ego. When George couldn't keep Angel anymore, Bill agreed to take her, but because she obeyed only Bill we had to keep her locked up above the kill room out back. Angel hated being in that room and would literally eat her way out of the second floor window, through glass and wood.

The first time Angel got out Bill was home and able to lock her up again.

"You need to get rid of that dog!" we all protested.

"The dog is staying, if you don't like it you can get the f*** out," he snapped back. Obviously, the dog was more important than his family.

A few weeks later, Angel got out again when Bill wasn't home. Pickles, our Dalmatian who'd recently had a litter of puppies, defended them against Angel and a chase ensued. As Angel chased Pickles, Tony, Sue, Uncle Skippy, JoJo, Carry, James and I chased both dogs. It was the biggest circus you've ever seen. There we were, running in the front door, through the house, exiting the side door off the kitchen and around again. We did this five or six times before things got bad. The screen door swung back and hit Carry in the face, breaking her nose and she started gushing blood. By then, Angel had Pickles pinned down and was literally ripping her neck off. Somehow Uncle Skippy was able to get Angel under control and tie her up to one of the cement blocks with a pole in the middle that we used for the cows. When Uncle Skippy turned to go into the house and get his gun, Angel started after him, dragging the cement block behind her.

"Shoot that dog!" we yelled.

He came out with a 357 Magnum and shot Angel. She continued coming after him as he kept shooting and shooting. He must have shot that dog six times before it finally died. When Bill came back, he was livid. It didn't matter that Carry had a broken nose or that Pickles had four gaping holes in her neck. He was pissed that we had to kill his dog. Later, after he calmed down a little he told us that he understood why we had to do it. Bill could go from being really pissed off to being extremely loving on a dime. One minute he'd call you a, "f****** retard" and the next he'd give you a big hug, saying, "Hey, baby give me a smooch."

Wearing one of Bill's black turkey farm logo tank tops and a pair of white shorts, I continued on my way, trying to find my brothers among the hundreds of people at the party. I noticed two guys hanging out by their truck, watching me. Never one to be shy, I decided to walk over and introduce myself. As I got closer, I could see that they were doing lines on the hood of the truck.

"Hey, guys," I said cheerfully. "What's up?"

"Not much, sweetness," one of the guys said as he stepped toward me seductively. He was clearly intoxicated and undressing me with his eyes.

"So what's your name, beautiful lady?" he asked.

"Jen," I responded. "What's yours?"

With the most horrified look on his face he said, "Not Bill's daughter, Jen!"

"Yeah," I replied, confused by the sudden change in his attitude.

Without hesitation, the two guys scooped up all their stuff and said, "We were warned to stay far away from you." With that, they hurried off and I never saw them again.

As I stood in disbelief at the whole scenario, I realized that Bill had apparently put out the word to stay away from his daughter; or else. Right at that moment Carry walked by with one of her childhood friends and noticed me. She immediately began going off about what I was wearing, saying it was too revealing.

"You're too young to be wearing that," she scoffed.

Having absolutely zero respect for her at that point, I just rolled my eyes, mumbled "bitch" under my breath and stormed off.

The friend Carry was with had been at the farm all week. Her name was Kelly and she had just lost her husband (his headless body had been recovered in some remote canyon). They had two little girls, aged five and seven. My heart went out to the kids because I knew how they must be feeling. But their mom was a whack job. A month or two after the party we found out that Kelly had been fooling around with her husband's best friend and together they had murdered him. When the cops caught on, Kelly and the boyfriend had taken off with the little girls. The week they'd stayed at the farm they were actually on the run. After they left they went out west somewhere and were living in a mineshaft for a few months before being caught. When they were captured, one of the little girls was found in the mineshaft bludgeoned to death.

Chapter Eleven

To those who didn't know about my life at the farm it appeared that I had everything: good looks, smart, friends and a boyfriend. But once I drove up that long dirt road, it was a different world: chores, lies, drugs and more chores.

Whenever James and I were at the farm, it was all about work, work, work. The privilege of participating in extra-curricular activities at school meant extra work on the farm. No one cared that James was on the football team and I was captain of the varsity cheerleaders, or that I was homecoming queen and on the honor roll. Those accomplishments were nothing more than a nuisance for Bill and Carry. They never said, "Hey we're really proud of you!" It was more like, "Great. Now you won't be around to do your chores." We had to "earn our keep," as Bill would say, and were supposed to be thankful that he put a roof over our heads.

Bill woke us up early, around six-thirty every morning. He didn't want anyone sleeping late, and if I didn't get up on the first call, he'd explode a quarter stick of dynamite out his window, which was right above mine. That happened only a few times before I learned to get moving once I heard his voice.

During the week I'd get ready and go to school and do my chores when I got home. But on the weekends, it was chores, chores, chores. Bill could always find something for us to do. It was around this time that James and I got really good at hiding. With a baggie of weed, we'd take our four-wheelers and head up to Pelican Point or ride out back behind the kill room away from the watchful eye of "Big Bad Billy D." When he would find us, he'd say, "What the f***! What are you f****** people doing? There's work to be done around here, goddamit!" As we scrambled to our feet, he would continue yelling, "You ungrateful little bastards! You don't know how good you have it. Most kids would kill to live like you."

Bill thought that just because we had four-wheelers and dirt bikes with hundreds of acres to ride them on that our life was perfect. If he only knew that we would gladly have given it all up for parents who talked to us and were excited about our accomplishments and things we were doing in school. Instead, Bill and Carry viewed us as just extra hands around the farm. Free labor!

While turkeys were the main asset to the farm, Bill continued to go through seasonal phases. We had four, big pot-bellied pigs and a bunch of piglets. One cold and rainy day they got out and Bill sent James, JoJo and me to catch them. Dressed in our yellow raincoats and mud boots, we spent the next couple of hours chasing them and trying desperately to return them to their pen. Bill stood on the porch yelling his orders on how we should be doing it and what we were doing wrong.

"Just corner them, you f****** retards," he hollered through all the commotion.

James, JoJo and I were covered in mud as we slipped and fell while attempting to capture them.

"Are you idiots?" he would rant when we got close enough to grab them, but missed.

They would slip through our hands, squeaking and squealing.

"Come out here and do it yourself, asshole," James said under his breath.

Eventually we got them all back in the pen, no thanks to Bill.

A few days later, our two new dogs, Bear Dog, who was a pit-bull and Shadow, a rottweiler got into the pigpen and ripped the hind quarters off them. The pigs were still alive but Bill had to put them down because they were so mangled. I held onto my little brother Jason, who was seven years old, shielding him from the gruesome sight while Bill shot them. He then aimed his 357 Magnum at Bear Dog and shot him in the head, then blew the rottweiler away, too. I thought that was a bit drastic, but that's how Bill was. It didn't matter that the dog belonged to James and that he had saved his money for months to buy it.

I turned and looked at James, in shock over what we'd just witnessed. I watched as another little piece of him died inside. Our bond was growing with every horrific event we endured and with each painful reminder of the day our lives changed forever. The place where everything was supposed to get better, where we could experience the innocence my mother so badly wanted for us, would prove to be the place we hated the most.

Once I turned sixteen and got my driver's license, Bill used our social security checks to buy a white utility van. It was supposedly for James and me, but it was mostly used for Bill's newest phase, produce runs. This was the only job we didn't have to help him with and the only one in which Bill had hands-on involvement, as it required driving to Boston every week. He would go down on Tuesday night and stay with a "friend." With orders he received from local restaurants in the surrounding towns, Bill would be at the Boston Market by 4:00 AM on Wednesdays, buy what he needed and come back to New Hampshire to deliver it.

Throughout high school James and I were each allowed to go out one night on the weekend, which meant we were constantly trying to decide if we wanted to go out Friday night or Saturday night. It made us angry to see all our friends having their entire weekends free while we had to choose which night we preferred to go out. Since we basically hung out with the same crowd, we would often pick the same night.

One Saturday night I wanted to go to a party. Because I'd already been out the night before, I knew it was pointless to ask permission to do so. My boyfriend Patrick was at this party. He called me a couple of times and I could hear everyone in the background hollering and having a good time. I also knew that a girl who really liked Patrick was at the party, and I worried that she would make a move on him if I wasn't around. Pacing back and forth in my bedroom as I spoke to Patrick on the phone, we began to devise a plan for my escape from the farm.

"Bill is asleep," I said to Patrick.

"Then come to the party for awhile," he said

"I don't know. I don't want to get in trouble," I replied.

"Jen, what teenager goes through high school and never sneaks out at least once?" Patrick said, trying hard to convince me to go.

"I guess I could take one of the trucks in the barn. No one would even hear me start it," I responded, a little apprehensive about disobeying Bill, who was asleep and would never even know I was gone. "Okay," I said excitedly "I'll be there in half an hour."

"Awesome," he said. "But be careful driving. It just started to snow and the roads might be slick."

Grabbing my jacket, I quietly climbed the stairs from my bedroom to the main floor. The living room was dark and the porch light was off, signaling that everyone in the house was in bed. The clock on the microwave oven said 10:05 PM. Slowly opening the front door, I stepped onto the front porch and saw that the snow had already started to accumulate.

Great! With my luck, I'll slide off the road and crash and then Bill will find out I snuck out.

I'd never had good luck; if I didn't have bad luck I'd have no luck at all. So with a sigh of resignation, I gave up and went back to my room and plopped down on my bed.

I was so much in love with Patrick during high school; he is the only person I ever regret lying to. After my mother's death, all my emotions shut down. But during my relationship with him, I felt things I'd never felt before and wouldn't feel again for years.

A few weeks after I chickened out of sneaking out of the house for the party, Patrick and I had dinner with his parents and two older brothers. It was the "meeting the parents, make a good-impression" dinner. His mother, a little German lady named Inga, took great pride in taking care of her husband and three sons. The epitome of an All-American-Family matriarch, she diligently prepared each person's plate, making sure they had everything they needed.

"Where do you live, Jennifer?" she asked me in a thick German accent as she placed a glass of milk in front of me.

"In Wentworth," I told her. I was so anxious to make a good impression that I didn't realize I was nervously picking at my left thumbnail, a habit I'd begun right after my mom died.

"Oh, you must live near the druggies and murderers at Bills Turkey Farm," she said matter-of-factly.

"Umm, no," I replied. "I live *at* Bills Turkey Farm."

The room went uncomfortably silent and I felt like I should explain myself further. But before I could say anything else the conversation quickly changed.

"More vegetables, William?" she asked, handing her husband a bowl of peas.

Looking over at Patrick for some reassurance that I hadn't just blown my first impression with his parents, he gave me a quick wink and started talking about the upcoming basketball game. As I sat quietly listening to Patrick and his family interact, I realized that this was what a real family was like. His parents were interested in what he was doing in school. They attended all of his sporting events and respected and listened to what he had to say. I desperately wanted them to like me but it was uncomfortable not knowing what they thought of me now that they knew where I lived.

It was around this time that I started hearing all the rumors that were circulating about Bill and the turkey farm. Until my junior year of high school, I'd never realized that anyone associated me with Bill. After all, he never came to a parent/teacher conference or to any function I was involved in. My last name was different from his. I never invited friends over and never, ever talked about anything that went on at the farm.

A few days later, Patrick broached the subject again. We were in his blue pickup truck driving home from the Concord Mall where we had been doing some Christmas shopping.

As our favorite song, *True Colors* by Cindy Lauper, played on the radio, Patrick turned to me and said, "Jen, I have a question and I want you to be totally honest with me."

"Okay," I responded.

"Don't get upset, but my mom heard a rumor from someone at work that Bill was a drug dealer. Is that true?"

Without hesitation I looked Patrick right in the eye and adamantly denied it. "Absolutely not," I said firmly. "He's a turkey farmer, you know that," I reminded him, clearly upset by the accusation.

"Alright, I believe you," he assured me. "I just needed to hear you say it."

Since we really did raise and slaughter turkeys, in my heart I wasn't totally lying. But I wasn't being completely honest, either. However, the truth always comes out, and eventually mine would, too.

Continuing north on Interstate 93, silence filled the car except for the faint sound of the radio. I was feeling guilty about lying to Patrick and wasn't in the mood to talk. He probably knew that I was bothered by the conversation and didn't want to make things worse. But when a news segment came on the radio reporting a drug bust in the southern part of New Hampshire, Patrick broke the silence.

"I think all drug dealers should be shot," he stated emphatically.

My face got hot and my blood started to boil as I defensively responded, "Drug dealers are just people trying to make a living and put food on the table like everyone else." By the time I realized what I was saying, it had already flown out of my mouth. And when I turned to look at Patrick, he had the most horrified look on his face. "I'm just saying," I fumbled, "you shouldn't judge someone until you've walked a mile in their shoes."

The Turkey Farm – Behind the Smile

    The stretch between Exit 23 and Exit 25 was long and uncomfortably quiet. With no street lamps on the New Hampshire highways, the only illumination came from random cars heading to the mountains to ski. I'm sure Patrick was wondering where my outburst had come from but he didn't say another word. I didn't want to make things worse, so I spent the remaining fifteen minutes before we reached his house gazing out the window and wondering why the justification I had used seemed to make sense only when Bill used it. My mind was swimming with fear that my secret life was slowly being revealed and there was absolutely nothing I could do about it.

    In the middle of my junior year, Bill and Carry had a son they named Jesse. It seemed my excruciating days working in the kill room slicing heads off turkeys, working in the gardens in the summer, cutting and stacking wood in the fall and cleaning the house year round weren't enough for them. Now I had to take care of their kid, too. Carry had post-partum depression and stayed in her bathrobe all day, hibernating in her bedroom and avoiding what little she did around the farm. As usual, I picked up the extra chores and now had the added task of making dinner for eight people every night. Somehow I managed to get my homework done and keep my grades up while playing wife and mother to everyone and still trying to be a typical teenager, too. It was insane! I started to resent Carry more and more but as always I smiled and did what I had to do to keep everyone happy.

Chapter Twelve

In February James and I spent our winter break in Florida with Nana and Pa. They had a time-share in Ormond Beach, a retirement community outside Daytona. We saw them only occasionally over the years, usually during school vacations, and rarely, if ever, did Jason come with us. I guess to them we were just painful reminders of the daughter they had lost. Nana and Pa rarely spoke of Mom and never asked any questions about Bill or what went on at the farm even though they were well aware of the environment we were exposed to.

When it came to my brothers and me, the orphaned children forced to grow up too fast, it was "out of sight, out of mind"—unlike the relationship Nana and Pa had with my cousins Jessica and Justin. Auntie Mary, Uncle Fred and their kids lived with my grandparents and were showered with the extra love and attention we never got. You'd think they'd want to compensate for the fact that we didn't have a mom, or a dad for that matter. But my relationship with my mother's family was superficial, to say the least. I know they loved us, but we never felt like a part of their family after Mom died.

James and I waited at the baggage terminal with Nana, who had come to pick us up. My suitcase had already come around, as did those belonging to the rest of the passengers on the plane. For ten minutes we waited, watching the empty carousel go around and around without James' bag. Unsure if it had been lost or confiscated I saw my brother turn white as he struggled to breathe. Worried I asked him if he was okay.

"I think I'm gonna be sick," he turned to me and said as he grabbed his stomach.

"It's okay, James. Your bag will come," I tried to reassure him, rubbing his back.

He started to sway back and forth and swallow repeatedly so I knew he was close to passing out.

"I'm so dead," he whispered, turning to me with fear in his eyes. I was beginning to panic myself when his lone navy blue duffel bag appeared. Relief replaced the grave look that had consumed him for what had felt like an eternity. James quickly grabbed his bag, which contained six joints stuffed beneath the insole of one of his sneakers, and hurried toward the door.

The weather wasn't very good during our stay in Florida, so we were bored most of the time. James and I walked along the beach and fed the seagulls and swam in the pool between rain storms to fill our time. Nana and Pa started their day with Bloody Marys at breakfast, then had wine with lunch and switched to highballs at five o'clock all while watching marathons of Wheel of Fortune and Jeopardy. When James and I were out of joints, we went down to the boardwalk and bought cigarettes from a vending machine at a bar.

"I can't wait to get home," James said one afternoon about four days into our trip.

"Me neither," I responded with a sigh, as my feet dangled off the wooden wharf. "I miss Patrick, and I can't believe we're already out of weed."

Throwing a piece of bread into the water, James jokingly said, "I wonder if someone from the farm would overnight us a couple of joints."

"Or maybe we could call Bill and see if he has any connections down here," I said, chuckling.

James grabbed the red pack of Marlboro cigarettes and lit one. "If we wait a couple more hours, Nana and Pa will be asleep and we can get into their booze."

"True, but we've never been much for drinking—not like most of our friends who go to parties for the sole purpose of getting drunk."

"Yeah, well, that's because Bill couldn't care less if we came home high. But God help us if we ever came home drunk."

"I guess at this point in our lives smoking weed is part of our genetic makeup," I said with a giggle.

That vacation with Nana and Pa marked the six-year anniversary of our mother's death. The month of February was always difficult for me. But, as usual, I put on a happy face and my big, bright smile and endured the week-long stay in the "white-head"-filled community, as James referred to it.

After landing at Logan airport in Boston the following Sunday evening, we went back to Nana's house, where Uncle Skippy was supposed to pick us up. When he hadn't arrived by nine o'clock, I knew he wasn't coming. That pissed me off because I was anxious to get home. Later that night, he called to say he would be there the next day, which ended up being late the following night. I was so angry that I didn't say one word to him the entire two-hour ride home, even when he passed me a joint hoping to lighten the mood. When we arrived at the farm, it was after midnight and I went straight to bed because I had school the next day and was already aggravated that I'd missed a day.

The next afternoon, Tuesday, March 3, 1987, I was driving my white van home from school. As I headed north on Route 25, I noticed several police cars, unmarked cars and mobile crime units parked in the Polar Caves parking lot. There must have been over fifty vehicles of various sizes with men in uniform suiting up.

"I wonder what's going on," I said to James, who was sitting next to me in the passenger seat.

"I don't know, but, man, someone's really screwed."

We arrived home and I immediately started preparing dinner and doing my homework at the same time (I had become very good at multitasking). Once supper was over and I'd cleaned up the dishes, I participated in our family tradition. Bill wasn't home, so Uncle Skippy did the honors.

We were no sooner finished when James walked past the front door and said, "There's a state trooper on the porch."

Because James was a proverbial joker, no one believed him. He liked to play practical jokes, like calling the farm and pretending to be the operator or saying that he was in the hospital with a broken leg. He would carry on so well that I believed him every time. I think it was James' humor that got him through our difficult and lonely childhood.

I thought this was just another one of his jokes until the front door flew open and a stream of policemen filed in. Over 500 DEA, FBI, state, local and federal officials came bursting through the heavy wooden door with guns and dogs. Standing frozen in the middle of the kitchen, I watched as they grabbed Uncle Skippy who was sitting on the wraparound couch. A cop came up behind him and flung him backwards onto the floor, frisking him for weapons. Others went into every room in the house with dogs, shouting "Seek drugs! Seek drugs!"

I watched out the kitchen window as hundreds of police officers walked side-by-side in a line across all five acres, looking for hidden people and drugs. The line of officers moved in perfect synchrony across the property toward the kill room located out back. There they found nothing more than the equipment used in the turkey processing plant, although they made a big deal about what they thought was a "secret room." It was nothing more than a studio apartment, but because it was behind two heavy barn doors they assumed it was hidden. Apparently, when adrenalin is your driving force, you can convince yourself of anything. These cops were bound and determined to get Bill.

Officers in the kitchen searched through cupboards, dumping sugar and flour on the counters and tasting it on their fingers (as if we'd keep drugs on the shelf with the spices!) I watched in horror as these men ransacked our house, pulling things out of drawers and lifting cushions.

An older man by the name of Lt. Brown eventually instructed me and my brothers to go into a back bedroom.

"May I pick up my little brother?" I asked, pointing to six-week-old Jesse, who was lying wrapped in a blanket in his basinet next to the coffee table. With the baby in my arms, we were led to James' room, where my cousin JoJo, 14, Jason, 8, James, 15 and I were left. The door was closed and an officer with rifle in hand stood guard. I don't know what they thought we'd do, but none of us said a word. For the next hour, we sat on the two twin beds listening to all the commotion.

In her long, blue plush bathrobe, Carry, who was still post-partum, was taken upstairs to the master bedroom. We could hear her crying hysterically as Lt. Brown yelled, "If you don't tell us where it is, we're going to start arresting those kids, starting with the oldest."

I looked at James whose eyes were wide with fear. Remembering what we had done right before they arrived, I discreetly began rubbing my fingers on the baby's blanket, hoping to erase any smell of marijuana.

We could hear the officers rummaging through bureaus and closets yelling out each find so it could be documented. On the left side of one bureau they found a jar containing approximately one pound of marijuana. A triple-arm weighing scale sat nearby with a large tray on top. Sitting next to it was Carry's pocketbook, which contained a baggie of pot.

"What's this?" the officer asked as he placed each item on the bed.

"It's for recreational use," she replied through sobs.

In another bureau they seized a bunch of photos of young and mature marijuana plants. One picture included Jason holding a bud. In the bottom drawer of another bureau were two baggies filled with marijuana seeds and several pipes.

"Quite the recreation," one of officers said sarcastically.

On the floor by the right side of the headboard was a brown paper bag with $21,000 in cash.

"This is a lot of money to be lying around, Carry. Any reason it's not in the bank?"

"I just haven't gotten around to depositing it," she said unconvincingly.

Another bureau contained two locked drawers. When the officers were unable to open the drawers, they yelled, "Where's the key, Carry?"

"I don't have it," she responded, sobbing uncontrollably again.

With that, the agents took a crowbar and popped the top of the bureau off to retrieve two more brown paper bags containing a total of $36,000, mostly in small bills.

"You might as well cooperate, Carry," Lt. Brown said. "Things will go a lot easier"

"I don't know what you're looking for," she yelled back.

"Where is he? Where's Bill," he shouted.

"What," Carry said with shock, "All this and you never thought to make sure Bill was here? He's sitting in the county jail in Boscown right now for traffic violations," Carry informed him with a laugh.

One of the officers pulled a bunch of ledgers out of the closet. He handed them to Lt. Brown who held them up to Carry's face and said, "This is all the proof we need, Carry, Bill is going down."

"Those are records for his business," she said, finding some momentary strength to defend her husband. "We have a thriving turkey business. That's all. And I'm not saying another word until I talk to my lawyer."

When Lt. Brown entered the bedroom where we were being held, he looked directly at me and said, "Jennifer, come with me."

Handing Jesse to James, I followed the lieutenant into the bathroom where he closed the door behind him. On the heels of my worst fear since my mother's death—getting arrested—I realized another fear: I could actually go to jail. Afraid that if I made eye contact I would reveal too much, I looked around the black-tiled bathroom with matching black sink and toilet. For wallpaper Bill had polyurethaned old newspapers onto the walls. He was eccentric like that.

"Has anyone in the house been smoking marijuana tonight?" Lt. Brown asked.

Remembering Uncle Skippy's instructions to put everything on him I responded, "My Uncle Skippy smoked outside earlier."

Of course that didn't explain the cloud of pot smoke that filled the living room, or the fact that my eyes were so red they looked like they were bleeding. I sensed he wasn't buying what I was saying. And then came the moment of truth.

"Can I smell your hand?"

Being left-handed, I gave him my right hand and watched as he brought it up to his nose.

"Now the other one," he commanded.

I lifted my left hand and turned my head away, hoping he wouldn't smell it if I wasn't looking. My heart was pounding so hard I thought it would come right out of my chest.

"Okay," was all he said before sending me back to the bedroom with the others.

When I returned to my brothers I could tell they were frightened beyond words—by the cops, and not knowing where I'd gone or if I was coming back. Since our mother's death I'd been the force behind our survival. They depended on me.

Shortly after my interrogation with Lt. Brown in the bathroom, we were ordered to gather some belongings. As two state troopers escorted me to my bedroom in the "forbidden" cellar, I heard another cop talking on the phone.

"She's not available right now and won't be back for a few days."

He must be talking to Patrick. He always called around this time, after basketball practice. How would I explain this to him, especially after promising him that everything his family had heard was a lie?

As I began packing a bag, one of the officers walked around my bedroom scanning everything from my homecoming queen tiara to the broken cigarette on the bureau.

"It's only a butt," I said as he picked it up and smelled it.

After placing it back in the ashtray, he walked over to the shelves that held all my awards.

"Seems you do very well in school," he commented, checking out all the trophies and ribbons proudly displayed above my desk. I'm sure the cops had a preconceived idea of what I must be like, based on what they'd been told before they even got to the farm.

"Were you here seven years ago?" I asked defensively.

"No."

"I was," the other officer responded. He was standing in the doorway at the bottom of the stairs.

"My mother's body was found right where you're standing," I said, nodding in his direction.

Uneasiness washed over him. Turning pale as though he were about to faint, he inched himself away from the area. Neither one of them said another word as I finished gathering my belongings.

When I returned to the living room, Carry's parents were waiting to take us to their house. Her mom was bundling Jesse into his car seat and JoJo was helping Jason pack up some toys. As a retired police officer, I'm sure Carry's father was rather uncomfortable being there while the farm was being raided. Without a word, he motioned for us to leave. As I walked down the steps of the front porch, Uncle Skippy and Carry were handcuffed and seated in the backseat of a cruiser. A federal agent was putting yellow "crime scene" tape around the perimeter of the house. James, who was in front of me, suddenly turned around and went back into the house, he emerged holding his blue evisceration jacket, which seemed odd to me, as he'd been wearing his ski jacket. Later that night I learned that the jacket he went back for contained a half-ounce of weed. I couldn't believe it. All those dogs and all those cops and no one found it.

On the way out of the driveway, the cruiser holding Carry and Skippy got stuck in the snow. Still handcuffed, Skippy was forced get out and push the police car. The wheels spun wildly as snow, salt and dirt sprayed back into his face. We watched as he rocked the car back and forth until it was free.

"Assholes," James mumbled under his breath as he descended the stairs to the waiting car.

Chapter Thirteen

I knew I had to tell Patrick. That night, when we got to Carry's parents' house, I called him and told him everything that had happened. I think it was too much for him to process all at once because he didn't have a whole lot to say to me that night, other than he was glad I was okay and that he'd see me at school in the morning. The next day at school I figured if I acted like nothing had happened no one would know. With my trademark smile and happy, upbeat personality, I was confident that no one would find out.

I never anticipated the magnitude of what had really happened or how newsworthy it was. It spread like wildfire, and by the time I got to school everyone knew. That morning, the bust was breaking news on WMUR-TV. It made the front page of every newspaper in the area, including the Union Leader. It was the biggest thing to hit Wentworth since my mother's murder. "Two arrested in Wentworth drug raid," one said. "Police haul marijuana out of home," another read. They made it sound like they'd cracked open a huge drug cartel. What they didn't print was the number of officers that were about to be demoted and/or fired because of their major screw-up.

The bust had been the culmination of a seven-year investigation. After my mother's death, the turkey farm and all its occupants had been under surveillance twenty-four hours a day, seven days a week. Our phones had been tapped and our vehicles followed. Even my white van had been followed. When I read that in the report with times and dates of when the van was seen parked at the top of Texas Hill Road I was horrified. That was where Patrick and I went to make out. Every move I had made since I was ten years old had been watched, listened to and documented. I felt as if I'd been living in a fishbowl. But, despite spending all that time and money trying to take down Bill, no one had thought to see if he would be home. Bill had been sitting in jail for two weeks.

Unfortunately for them the Feds were also a day late. The person who'd ratted on Bill to begin with developed a guilty conscience and called Carry to inform her that the farm was about to be busted. That was why Skippy hadn't come to pick James and me up at our Nana's when he was supposed to after our trip to Florida. He had a lot of cleaning to do.

The one thing that really pissed me off about the report I'd read was that the cops referred to Bill's turkey business as "menial," a mere hobby at best, only used as a front for his drug business. My years of fourteen-hour days doing hard labor on that farm beg to differ!

Still, I worried about how people would react. Although everyone knew about the turkey farm, and that I lived there up until then they'd never really associated me with it or Bill. We had different last names and Bill had attended none of my school functions or parent/teacher conferences. He was my provider, not my parent.

I was amazed by the amount of support and encouragement I received. My English teacher approached me in the hall and said, "If you need anything at all, someone to talk to or a place to stay, you can come to me." She never mentioned the bust or what she knew; just that she was there if I needed her.

Later that day, I was standing in the lobby with a group of friends when another friend came over and said, "My mother told me to tell you that you're always welcome at our house but that I was *never* allowed to go to yours."

I just laughed because even before the bust I'd never wanted my friends to come to the "freak farm" anyway. James and I liked to keep our social life separate from the farm.

For me, the worst thing about the bust was that my secret was out. I was mortified when every member of Patrick's family called to ask what had happened. They were concerned about me and wanted to know if I was okay, but Patrick's parents still wanted him to break up with me. They didn't want their son associating with me because of Bill and the farm. Patrick was contemplating it, not because of the bust but because I had lied to him. He was hurt that I hadn't told him the truth when he first asked, and he felt like he couldn't trust me. After reassuring him that I was sorry and would never be dishonest with him again, we managed to work through this major problem. Things were strained for awhile but eventually Patrick's parents accepted the fact that we were going to stay together and they grew to love me like a daughter.

Carry distanced herself from everyone after the bust. The cops didn't get enough to hold charges against her and Uncle Skippy, so they were released. Still, Carry was embarrassed by what the townspeople thought. She started sending me to school functions with Jason because she couldn't face all the locals. Everyone regarded Bill as some horrible criminal who made his living by dealing drugs, and the rumors got worse. Even though they lived in Massachusetts, I know Auntie and my grandparents heard about the bust. But, as usual, they turned a blind eye and never asked any questions.

To the Feds' chagrin, the guns that were seized were the only thing they were able to get on Bill. Because he hadn't filed the proper paperwork when he was a teenager in Massachusetts, he was still considered a felon in possession of firearms. It didn't matter that twice before—once when my mom was killed and once when Bill had a fight with Tony—the cops had taken and then returned the guns, unaware of his record. The Feds went to Bill several times while he was in jail for the traffic violations and offered him early release if he would roll over on a couple of his buddies who had recently been busted for drugs.

"Nope, I think I'll just stay here," Bill said.

His minimum thirty-day stay for the traffic violations was increased to the maximum of one year. He would still have to serve time for the gun charges at a later time.

For a brief moment I was proud of Bill. By refusing to squeal on someone else in order to save is own ass proved his loyalty, and that said a lot. As far back as I can remember, Bill had always told me, "There's nothing worse than a rat." It's ingrained in my soul and I believe that way to this day.

Over the next four months, while waiting approval for work release, Bill insisted that someone from the farm come to see him every visiting day— Tuesday, Thursday and Sunday. Usually James and I went, but not because we wanted to. The bust had really affected Carry and she'd become a recluse. We were searched each time we walked through the metal detector. In the visiting room (which was also the cafeteria) were four lines of long brown tables with built-in seats. The inmates sat on one side, visitors on the other.

After we updated Bill on everything that was going on at the farm, he would tell us stories about some of the other inmates. The minimum security guys who got work detail at the county farm would arrange for their girlfriends to meet them wherever they were working. They'd run off somewhere to have sex, then the girlfriends would leave and the guys would finish their work before going back to the jail. It was all about what they could get away with.

I'll never forget this one incident; it's etched in my memory bank as a reminder of how *not* to become—weak and submissive to a man. During one visit, this grungy-looking guy suddenly grabbed his girlfriend by the wrist and pulled her toward him with his other hand around her neck. Startled, I watched as the guard just sauntered over and said, "Alright, alright, visit's over" and broke them up. Well, if I didn't see her back the next week with a broken wrist and bruises all over her neck! I was horrified.

When Bill got work release halfway through his jail time, he was allowed to come home Monday through Friday from 8:00 AM to 5:00 PM. Uncle Skippy would pick him up and I would take him back. For six months

I had to add to my already-full day driving forty-five minutes, each way, to take Bill back to jail every evening.

One spring afternoon when Bill was home on work release, I was sitting in the living room choosing courses for my senior year. Bill happened to be in the room and asked me what I was doing.

"I'm picking out my classes for next year," I told him.

Picking up my schedule, he started to scrutinize it. "You should have taken Marketing," he said. "And what the hell are you thinking, not taking Economics?"

I couldn't believe him! He'd never once showed an interest in what I was doing in school. I was about to be a senior in high school and this was the first time he'd ever asked me about my courses.

"I'm getting ready to graduate, and now you suddenly take an interest in what I do in school," I snapped at him. "All my classes have been college prep."

He threw my schedule down on the couch and sneered, "You're not worth the shit that comes out your ass. You think you can get into college. Who the f*** do you expect to pay for it?"

Furious that he could turn a simple task into such a painful experience, I screamed back at him, "You make me wish I was dead instead of my mother."

"You little bitch!" Bill spat as he walked away. "I should have given you back when I had the chance."

Fuming, I stormed down to my bedroom and threw myself across the bed. Tears were something I hadn't shed since my mother's funeral, but Bill had made me so angry I felt like bawling. Instead of giving in to my emotions, though, I lit up the half-joint sitting in my nightstand. Within a few minutes I felt much better and could face the rest of the day, including taking Bill back to jail a few hours later.

My senior year of high school was relatively event free. While my secret was now out teachers, friends and parents didn't treat me any differently. In fact, I give credit to them for being the reason I got through it all. My chores and responsibilities around the farm stayed the same but the activities and amount of people diminished after the bust. I didn't really see pot around, at least not in the quantities I did before. Bill still had his own personal stash in the house and James and I continued to steal from it.

Contrary to the feds belief the turkey business continued to thrive and Bill now offered smoked turkeys to customers. Rumor was that people could buy a turkey stuffed with pot instead of giblets but that wasn't true. The smoked turkeys required Uncle Skippy, JoJo, James and me to drive down to Shaker Village in Canterbury, New Hampshire a couple of nights a week after killing turkeys all day to have them smoked before packaging them. Often it was after nine o'clock at night before we even got there and it took a couple of hours to have them smoked. Then we'd have to drive over an hour to get home. "Kill" season was the most exhausting time of year for me.

Chapter Fourteen

Graduating from high school in June of 1988 was the beginning of a whole new life. I couldn't wait to move off the farm and away from Bill and Carry. And I swore that once I left I was *never* coming back.

My time at Plymouth State College, 1988-1989, in Plymouth, New Hampshire was nothing more than one big party and a chance to find my own identity outside the farm. I was free to go out with my friends every night if I wanted to, so I did. The weekend started on Thursday night. My new friends would gather in my dorm room for "happy hour" before hitting the fraternity parties.

Of course, the most common questions people asked when they first met me were: Where are you from? What do your parents do? I suppose I could have chosen to lie or vaguely say that my mother was dead and my step-dad was a turkey farmer. But instead, I felt the need to be truthful and share the details of my childhood with those closest to me at the time. For the first time I could speak freely and honestly about my mother's death and the events that had shaped my life.

But as I spoke about my childhood, it became surreal and seemed more like a movie I'd watched than the life I'd lived. Their reactions and responses forced me to become painfully aware of my lack of emotion. It was during this time that my level of deprivation became clear. Sure I had "things"—food, clothes, toys, trips. But I lacked what was most important: emotion and feeling. Towards the end of high school, my knowledge of this had become increasingly evident, but it wasn't until college that it began to really affect me.

Sprawled out on the floor drinking gin and tonics one night, the conversation evolved into one of those impromptu bonding sessions where each person would share something about themselves that was secret. Most of the girls would talk about the things they did in high school that their parents didn't know about, like the first time they had sex or what drugs they tried. For whatever reason—maybe it was the fact that I'd had a few drinks—I wanted to shock them. So I told them the short version of my childhood and what my life had been like to that point.

"Yea, mine was just your average childhood. My mother was murdered, my real dad is a drunk, my step-dad was a drug dealer and my family was under a seven-year federal investigation before my house got busted at gunpoint.

"Holy shit, Jen! Did that really happen to you?" my roommate Julie asked.

"It most certainly did," I said with a chuckle, noticing the tears in her eyes. I was suddenly uncomfortable but didn't want any of them to notice, so with a swig of my drink, I said, "Aw, it's all good. What doesn't kill you makes you stronger."

"Jesus Christ suffered as much as you, but at least he had a family who loved him," my friend Amy said, openly crying but trying to laugh with me.

"You should be so messed up," another girl, Christy, said.

"How can you be so cavalier about all this?" my roommate asked as the others looked on with a combination of horror and pity.

"Normal is what you know, that's just the way my life was. I can't change the cards that were dealt, but I can control how I let it affect me," I said casually.

"Wow, you're amazing, Jen!" Amy spoke again. "If all that had happened to me, I would be locked up in a psychiatric ward somewhere."

Speaking openly and honestly about my mom and the farm was a release, but it was nothing compared to how I felt seeing my friends cry about things I'd never, myself, cried about. One of the benefits of living away from the farm was that it allowed me the opportunity to finally process my mom's death. As the feelings I had suppressed for years slowly began to surface, I realized it had been easier to go through the motions, speaking without feeling, than face the reality that I may have emotional issues, especially about losing my mom. Hiding deeper behind my smile, I figured the more I laughed and entertained people, the less likely my past would matter. The more friends I had, the more accepted I felt, so I made sure I was always the life of the party. I was game for anything and excitement followed me. But I felt increasingly hollow inside. My soul burned with questions, and my desire for answers began to haunt me.

As horrible and tragic as my mother's murder was I always thought I knew the details and truth behind it. Turns out I knew only what was appropriate for a ten-year-old to hear. For most people that would have been enough, but it wasn't for me. I needed to know more.

One crisp October afternoon, I ditched my psychology class and went to the library on campus. Locating the section that housed the microfiche in the back corner of the building, I proceeded to look up the newspaper articles regarding my mother's death. For over two hours I read everything I could find. Even though I already knew the basic information about my mom's murder – that Suds stabbed her thirty-one times in front of my little brother – the freedom of finally being able to learn the details fueled my need to know why. The only person who could tell me was the man responsible for my mother's death: Steven "Suds" Sudvari.

Mustering up my courage, I sat down and wrote a very short but concise letter, stating only that I was the oldest child of Patricia Keefe and that I wanted to meet with him. A few weeks later, I received a letter explaining the process I had to go through in order to visit him. Because I was a relative of the victim, this included a meeting with the warden. Keeping my secret, I began the necessary steps through the prison to obtain clearance for a visit.

I always told myself and my brothers that when I turned eighteen, I would leave the farm and never come back. When I left for college, I swore I would never kill another turkey as long as I lived. But somehow, through guilt and a little bribery, Bill managed to get me back for one more kill season. So much for breaking free from the imprisonment of the farm and Bill!

Wanting to maintain what little control over my life I'd gained since leaving for school, I decided to torture Bill a bit. While at the farm working my last kill season, I said matter-of-factly, "I wrote a letter to Suds and I'm going to the prison to meet with him."

Bill removed a pack of Marlboros from his shirt pocket, took out a cigarette and lit it. He looked me square in the eye for a few minutes before he got up from the table and left the room without saying a word. His reaction surprised me. It wasn't like him to avoid a confrontation or the opportunity to speak his mind. Even though I wouldn't let him influence my decision, I was curious to know what he thought about my pursuit to see Suds. But he never said a word, not even a few weeks later when I went back for Thanksgiving dinner.

During winter break, I was forced to move back to the farm for a few weeks. The college closed the dorms over the holiday and no one was permitted to stay. But I didn't go without a fight.

"I'll do anything," I begged the resident advisor at my dorm.

"My hands are tied, Jen," she said sympathetically.

"I can't go back to that farm," I said desperately. "Isn't there someone I can plead my case to? I'll work. I'll clean the common areas. I'll pay you whatever you want."

Her eyebrows knit together. "Damn, girl. Is it really that bad at home?"

I had her attention and thought I might be able to persuade her to let me stay. "You have no idea," I responded.

"I wish I could help you, but there are no exceptions. Isn't there a friend you could stay with, or some other option?"

The only person I knew I could have stayed with was my best friend from high school, Sha, but she had moved to California after graduation. Knowing there was nothing I could say that would convince her to let me stay at the dorm over winter break, I hung my head in defeat. "That's okay. I understand. Thanks anyway."

Having no other choice, I reluctantly went home. *It's only for four weeks. How bad could it really be?* But I should have known better. At the farm it was always bad. And that time, I had an eerie feeling, an uncomfortable uneasiness that I couldn't place or shake.

The first two weeks of my stay back at the farm weren't too bad. Turkey season had come to an end. After the bust more than a year and a half earlier, Bill had begun to scale back on his other phases and only the produce runs remained in operation. Carry had even mellowed out a little and was taking more responsibility for Jesse, who was now a very active toddler. James and Jason were happy to have me home again, so I seized the opportunity to spend quality time with them before going back to the dorm in mid-January.

Bill and I didn't say anything more about my setting up a meeting with Suds at the prison. I couldn't help but wonder what he was thinking but was afraid to broach the subject again. Maybe the tide was turning and he was beginning to realize I was old enough to control my own life and he couldn't interfere anymore.

But reality hit one afternoon when I went to campus to check my mail. There was a letter from Suds that simply said, "The conditions in the prison have changed. Please don't contact me again." As I stood outside the dorm and read the letter over and over again, shock turned to disappointment then anger. In that moment, I realized that Bill did have something to say after all, and this was his way of saying it. I knew he'd made contact with some of his buddies who were incarcerated and gotten word to Suds not to meet with me. Knowing Bill, I had no doubt that some heavy threats had been used to make his point. I couldn't help but recall the time I asked Bill after my mother's funeral what would have happened if he had found Suds before the cops did.

"He would have gotten a brand new pair of cement shoes," was all he said.

When I got back to the farm I was so pissed at Bill I couldn't even look at him. I knew it would be pointless to say anything because he'd probably just deny it. There was no point in defending my need to find answers and bring closure to my mother's death. He would do what he always did and twist things around to somehow make me feel like I'd done something wrong. Every time I tried to talk about my mom, and her death, Bill would shut me down. I wanted to know the details and truth about what had happened the night she was murdered. What was he hiding? I decided to make the best of the remainder of my time at the farm but swore to myself that I would never, ever come back. I was finished with Bill and his sick, twisted ways.

Christmas vacation was over for my little brothers and they had school the next day, so they had to go to bed early. I didn't want to be left alone with Bill for fear I might weaken and confront him, so I went to bed when they did, praying the rest of my stay would be without incident.

But at five o'clock the next morning we were woken up with guns in our face and the cops saying, "Okay, kids, it's time to get up for school now."

As I opened my eyes, two officers were standing over me, each with a rifle pointed at me. *Not again*, I thought. I could hear scurrying going on upstairs and Bill yelling, "What the f*** is going on?" Scrambling out of bed, I followed the officers upstairs where the rest of my family was gathered in the living room. The familiar looks on my brothers' faces tore at my heart. Bill was standing in the kitchen with Lt. Brown, who informed him, "Well, Mr. Dalton, the federal government now owns this property."

"This is bullshit," Bill spat as he grabbed the papers that were being served to him.

"It seems you've made a lot of money over the years but failed to file tax returns," Lt. Brown responded.

This time there were only about fifty officers. After they gave Bill the news that the farm was being seized (it would be almost two years before he had to move out) they left. While my brothers went to school, I listened to Bill whine and pity himself for all he'd lost. I wondered if he even thought about how much my brothers and I had lost, which was so much more than mere possessions. We'd lost our mom and our childhood. We'd worked just as hard, if not harder. For eight years, we'd put our blood, sweat and tears into building that farm, and all Bill could do was think of himself. If you asked him we hadn't done enough; all he cared about was how much more we could have done to help out. Bill refuses to see certain things and figures if he doesn't talk about it, it doesn't exist—even my mother's murder. Bill has been able to justify in his own mind why he bares no guilt or blame for what happened to her.

Even though I hated the farm for what it represented, my dream was to turn it into something positive in memory of my mother. My hope was to someday own it and keep it as a working farm for underprivileged kids.

Chapter Fifteen

In an effort to find answers and bring closure to my haunting questions, I traveled back to the Grafton County courthouse. The long, desolate drive was still familiar, even though it had been eight years since the trial of my mother's killer.

Upon entering the courthouse, I was overcome by a wave of nausea. The metal detector beeped as I went through.

"Please step over here, ma'am," the officer said. After outlining my body with a wand- shaped metal detector, he told me I could proceed.

"I'm looking for Court Records," I said.

"It's right over there," he replied, pointing in the direction I needed to go.

As I entered the office, an older brunette lady got up from her desk and walked over to the counter. "May I help you?" she asked cordially.

"I'd like to see transcripts for a case from 1981, The State of New Hampshire vs. Steven Sudvari." I wondered if she could sense my nervousness.

After writing down the information, she looked up and said, "I'll be right back."

About fifteen minutes later she returned, her arms loaded with the bound transcripts, eight in all.

"Sorry it took so long, I had to go to the basement to retrieve them," the woman said.

I sat down at a tiny cubicle in the corner of the room and took a deep breath, preparing myself for what I would soon learn about my mother's death and the man responsible.

The first folder I opened was prosecutor Attorney Roudes' opening statement at the start of the trial.

"Members of the jury, you will hear testimony today about the defendant, Steven Sudvari. You will hear the details about how distraught he was when his girlfriend left him shortly before the night in question, February 26, 1981. You will hear that he worked for Bill Dalton on the day that Patricia Keefe was killed. You will also hear testimony from friends of Patricia and they will describe for you a lifestyle that is perhaps very different from your own. It is important for you to keep in mind as you listen to these witnesses that in a case like this the State cannot choose its witnesses and cannot change their backgrounds to make them more acceptable to you. I ask you to judge their credibility in light of what you will learn about them during the course of their testimony."

At that moment I realized that in the pursuit of justice and punishment, my mom's friends had been willing to be honest about their illegal drug use, even if it meant incriminating themselves. I would always remember the integrity they displayed as each one depicted honestly what had happened the night before my mom died.

The first person to take the stand was one of my moms best friends, Linda. As I read her testimony, I could picture her in my mind. She was a petite woman with shoulder-length, light brown hair. I remember Linda as the emotional, bubbly one who was always dependent on a man.

"Can you please tell the court your relationship with the victim."

"She was my best friend," Linda stated. "We'd been friends since grade school.

"And your relationship to the defendant?"

"I knew him from working for Bill and Patty on the farm."

"Would you please tell the court what you were doing the day before Patricia Keefe was killed."

"On Wednesday, February 25, 1981 there was a huge snowstorm and the power was out. Patty asked us to come over because she didn't want to be alone with her small son."

"When you got to the farm, who was there?"

"Patty, her son Jason, the defendant Suds and Bill's assistant Alvin."

"Who was with you?"

"My husband Doug."

"What were the occupants in the house doing?"

"Patty was in the kitchen, and Alvin and Suds were sitting on the couch."

"Did you observe anything unusual?"

"Yes, I did. Suds' speech was broken and he was saying, 'I'm really screwed up right now, really f*** up.' He just didn't act normal. I asked Patty what was wrong with Suds."

"Do you know what caused the defendant to act that way?" the attorney questioned.

"Yes. Patty told me he'd taken a hallucinogen called PCP."

"After you entered the house and saw the defendant acting in such a way, what did you do then?"

"I took off my jacket, went into the kitchen with Patty and made a drink and then sat down in the living room."

"What kind of drink did you make?"

"I can't recall. Something with vodka and maybe orange juice or grapefruit juice."

"During the course of the evening, did you ingest anything else?"

"Yes, I did," Linda answered as she cleared her throat.

"What was that?"

"I smoked some marijuana."

"Did you take anything else?"

"I took some cocaine," she continued.

"How much cocaine did you take?" attorney Roudes pressed.

"I probably did around five lines over the course of seven hours or so."

At that point the judge said, "Thank you for your honesty, but can I stop you here for a minute? Could you please tell us exactly what the word 'line' means?"

"Oh, it's just how you put cocaine on a mirror to snort it," Linda said matter-of-factly before she went on to detail her recollection of what had happened that night.

"As the snow piled up around the house, Karen and her husband Peter came by to spend the night. They were going to Boston with Patty the next day to help a friend move. The house was lit by candles and kerosene lamps because the electricity had gone out. Patty cooked dinner on the woodstove. She made spareribs, baked potatoes and salad. From the time I originally got to the house around 3:00 PM until approximately 9:00 PM that night, Suds stayed in the same position on the couch, unable to move because he was so messed up. He passed out for a while at one point and little Jason crawled up on the couch beside him and fell asleep. Everyone was eating when Suds awoke. When he saw the baby next to him, he started freaking out because he thought he had killed Jason. Doug got up and went over to Suds and said, 'It's okay, man, he's only sleeping.' After that, Suds settled back down on the couch and stayed there a while longer."

"What was the defendant drinking that night?" attorney Roudes asked

"Coca-Cola."

"Was there any alcohol in it?"

"No."

"How do you know?"

"Because he kept asking me to taste it before he would drink it because he was afraid there might be alcohol in it."

"Why didn't he want to drink alcohol?"

"Suds was paranoid about drinking. He told us that it had been a very long time since he had drunk and didn't want to start now. He said alcohol made him volatile. We actually got into a discussion about whether alcohol was a disease or an addiction. Patty even got out a dictionary to look up the definition."

"What happened next?"

"Suds became very angry when she read the true definition because he was wrong about it being an addiction. He started getting loud and I couldn't tell if he was yelling or just talking loud. He still couldn't get off the couch because he was so messed up but his behavior changed after that. He became bitter and argumentative. I'd never seen him that way before. I just attributed it to him being so messed up on drugs and about Cathy leaving him."

"How did you know he was more messed up on drugs this time than in the past?"

"I could tell that his depth perception was way off. Every time he wanted a cigarette I had to light it for him and each time I did he thought I was trying to burn his face. He thought I was a lot closer then I really was."

"Did the defendant change position at all during the time you were at the house?"

"Only once, when he had to go to the bathroom and he needed help because his legs were like rubber."

"Who helped him?"

"Doug assisted him. He took him by the arm and led him into the bathroom. As he was doing that, Patty, Karen and I tried to lighten his mood by singing a Beatles song, *I Get By With a Little Help From My Friends*. After Doug left the bathroom, Suds yelled out some sexually explicit comments, but we just laughed and told him to pull up his pants and come out of the bathroom. It was all in fun."

"Did you see the defendant take any more substances that night?"

"No. Doug and I left around 11:30 PM."

"I have no further questions," attorney Roudes said, and Linda was told she could step down.

Flipping through the transcripts, the next testimony I read was Nard's. She hadn't been at the farm the night in question but had received a phone call from Suds the day after my mom was killed. She was also the first one to go to the hospital and see Jason.

Nard was also asked her full name and relationship to the victim.
"She was my best friend," Nard answered. "We've known each other since we were kids. I miss her very much."
"On the morning of Thursday, February 26, 1981, did the victim Patricia Keefe call you on the phone?"
"Yes, she did," Nard replied.
"Do you recall what time it was?"
"Around twelve-thirty in the afternoon, I think."
"What did she say?" attorney Roudes continued.
"She asked me if I wanted to come over. She said that she was going to take Jason sledding for a little while and then she would be home."
"What did you say?"
"I told her I had a flat tire and couldn't come," Nard said.
"Did she sound like anything was wrong?"
"No. She said she was going to call her big kids who were in Massachusetts with their dad and then she was going to clean up the house before taking Jason to play in the snow. I asked her why she didn't go to Boston with Doug and Linda."
"And what was her response?"
"She said that she was too tired because everyone had come over the night before and they went to bed late and she didn't feel like getting up early and driving two hours."

"Did you receive a phone call from the defendant in the early morning hours of Friday, February 27, 1981?" the attorney asked.

"Yes, I did."

"Can you tell the court what was said during that conversation?"

"The telephone rang around two-thirty in the morning. I usually wouldn't get up if it rang in the middle of the night like that; I figure if it's important they'll call back. But something told me to get up and answer it. When I picked up, I almost couldn't even recognize the voice. He was screaming frantically into the phone."

"Who was?"

"Suds. He said, 'I killed her, Nard. I killed Patty.'"

"Not sure what was going on, as I tried to wake up I asked him what he was talking about," Nard continued to tell the court. "Suds went on yelling into the phone, 'I'm surprised you haven't found her. I didn't mean to hurt the baby. Someone needs to go check on the baby.' I asked him, 'Why, Suds? Why?' Suds said, 'That's the same thing Patty asked me.' Then his voiced changed from hysteria to pure evil and he said into the phone, 'I didn't kill her. I butchered the bitch.'

"Still unsure what was going on, I called Linda and told her that she needed to send Doug to the farm to check on Patty and Jason. She told me that he was already on his way up there because they had received a call from the police wondering why their Bronco was abandoned in West Lebanon, thirty miles away. She went on to tell me that she and Doug had left it at the farm the day before and taken one of Bill's trucks with them to Boston. When I told Linda about the phone call I received from Suds, she became frantic and said that she would call the officer that had phoned them about the Bronco."

"After you received the call confirming your fear that Patty was dead, what did you do?"

"I immediately went to the hospital to see baby Jason."

"When you entered the hospital room, where was Jason?"

"He was sleeping in a nurse's arms."

"What did you do?"

"I went over and took him out of her arms and sat down in the rocking chair next to the window, where I stayed for the next few hours waiting for Bill to return from his 'business' trip."

"Did anyone else come and see Jason?" the attorney questioned.

"A detective came in and gave him a piece of paper and a pencil."

"What did Jason do with it?"

"At first he didn't do anything. But later he took it and started poking holes in the paper saying, 'stab it with a knife…..stab it with a knife.' Later the detective came back, I assume to see if Jason had drawn anything, and when he saw all the holes he asked me how it happened."

"Was that all?"

"No. Jason was lying on my chest with his thumb in his mouth as I sang and rocked him. The detective asked Jason if he knew who hurt him. Eyes wide with fear, Jason took his thumb out of his mouth and said, 'Suds hurt my mommy and made her bleed.' Then he put his thumb back in his mouth and nestled against me and closed his eyes."

As I read this, I could picture my little brother, a chubby two-and-a-half-year-old with big chocolate eyes and jet-black hair. It broke my heart to think of what Jason had gone through and how those horrific images were locked somewhere in his memory, unable to surface. I thought about what the nurses who worked in the emergency room the morning he was brought in must have felt seeing this little boy, knowing the horror he had witnessed. I wondered how Nard must have felt, thinking that if she had gone over to the farm that day my mom might still be alive.

The next testimony I read was Doug's. His early questioning just reiterated what Linda had stated about the night before my mother's death. But then he was questioned about how he found her when he went to the farm on the early morning of February 27, 1981.

"I arrived at the farm at approximately three o'clock in the morning. It was pitch black. There were still no lights on in the house and there was no smoke coming out of the chimney. I thought that was odd because I had distinctly told Suds to keep the woodstove going. There were no vehicles in the driveway and my Bronco was not in the barn where I had left it the day before. With only the light from my BIC lighter, I walked into the house from the side door, which enters the kitchen, and called Patty's name, but there was no answer. Again, I thought that was odd because she told Linda and me the day before that she wasn't going anywhere. Jason's riding toy lay in the middle of the floor and I almost tripped on it in the darkness.

"Suddenly, a small, faint voice echoed in the darkness. 'Doug, help me!' I couldn't tell where it was coming from. Walking through the main floor checking both bedrooms, I followed the voice to the bathroom. That is where I found Jason, barely conscious and lying on the floor in only his underwear. He had wrapped a few towels around him to keep warm. When I scooped him up, I noticed blood dried on the side of Jason's face and a sick feeling came over me. Placing him on the couch and covering him with warm blankets, I yelled again for Patty but got no answer. As I looked out the living room window, I could see a light flickering outside. I went to the front door and saw a dark figure walking up the driveway. Being a Vietnam Vet, my defense mechanism kicked in and I positioned myself firmly on the porch.

"At that point I was still unaware that Suds had called Nard but was highly suspicious of what I had found at the farm so far. 'Who's there?' I yelled to the person walking toward the house. Officer Smith identified himself. Due to the massive amount of snow that had fallen the day before, he had to park his cruiser at the bottom of the driveway. He walked toward the door with his hand on the gun belted to his hip. He told me he had phoned dispatch to have an ambulance and backup units put on standby and then explained why. I let him know that I also had a gun, and he assured me that he was okay with that. He informed me that he knew I'd be up there and that Linda had called and asked him to come too.

"With no sign of Patty, Officer Smith and I began to search the rest of the house. We checked the master bedroom, but she wasn't there. As we descended the spiral stairs, Smith pointed his flashlight to the floor and we noticed a large pool of blood next to the woodstove. I knew instinctively that this was not going to be good. Looking over at Jason still on the couch, eyes wide with shock, my heart sank. He looked at me and then at the area where the light shone.

"Officer Smith continued down the stairs that would bring him to the basement. He stopped and tried to prevent me from coming any further but it was too late. The light from his flashlight was shining on Patty's lifeless body. She was lying face-up at the bottom of the stairs, her head resting on the last step. I've seen some awful things in my life, especially over in 'Nam, but nothing prepared me for such a gruesome sight. And of someone I loved like a sister. I fell to my knees and sobbed, for myself, for her, for her children. The loss those kids would feel....I just miss her so much."

When I finished reading Doug's testimony, my face was wet with tears. I hadn't even realized I was crying. I couldn't wrap my mind around what he must have felt at the moment he came upon my mother's body.

After perusing through testimonies from other witnesses, I searched for the one I wanted to read most—that of the man responsible for taking my mother away. I didn't need any more details of how she died; I wanted to know *why*.

Flipping through the blue bound transcripts, I searched for Suds' explanation of what had happened. The first line of questioning provided background information. Suds explained that he had moved to New Hampshire from Pennsylvania in the summer of 1980 and that he started to work for Bill a few months later. He was paid $3.50 an hour cleaning chicken shit and doing odd jobs around the farm. He told the court that he was on probation in Pennsylvania for theft and that in the month prior to the night in question he'd found out there was a warrant for his arrest for failure to pay restitution.

"My probation officer told me that if they found me I would definitely be going back to jail," Suds told the court. "I wasn't particularly enthused by that information. That, plus the fact that my old lady left me had me pretty pissed off."

"What did you do after you found out there was a warrant for your arrest?" the prosecuting attorney asked.

"Patty suggested I try to find help—counseling or something. She said that there was an outreach program in Manchester for Vietnam Veterans and that maybe they could help me transfer my probation to New Hampshire and work out a deal so that I wouldn't have to go back to jail."

"Did you contact the VA?"

"Yeah, but it was a bunch of bullshit. It was nothing but a lot of Jesus freaks, so I stopped the process."

"What happened after you stopped attending the meetings?" attorney Roudes asked.

"I just didn't want to deal with it. I didn't care anymore. I smoked marijuana extensively and used caffeine pills to keep going."

"Is this your normal habit?"

"I would have to say my usual routine is to take a couple caffeine pills in the morning when I get up and then smoke a joint. Then smoke another joint on my way to work at seven o'clock in the morning. Probably around ten o'clock in the morning I would smoke another joint, and somewhere in the vicinity of noon I would smoke another. Around two o'clock I would take a brake and smoke another joint. That was my daily routine. I probably took over a dozen valiums and maybe three Percodans over the period of a month before the night I killed Patty."

"So you admit to killing Patricia Keefe on February 26, 1981?"

"Yes, sir."

"Do you recall the day before, the day that everyone partied at the residence of Patty?"

"Yes, I do."

"Is the testimony you have heard fairly consistent with your memory?"

"Some of it, yes."

"What do you remember about the party?"

"At approximately four o'clock in the afternoon, Patty asked me if I would like to do some PCP. She said that it was stale and that it probably wasn't going to be very potent but that I could have it. I hadn't done PCP in years, since Vietnam, but I figured what the hell. My life kind of sucks right now; I'd like to forget about it for awhile. I took the brownish stone and cut two large lines. Patty said she didn't want any and that I could have all of it. I snorted the lines and waited to see how it was going to affect me before doing any more. It wasn't stale, I'll tell you that. After about an hour, I couldn't even walk and just sat on the couch. I could hardly even talk. I remember seeing Doug and Linda come in, but I don't know what time it was. My visual patterns were way off. Some things seemed far away, and other times it seemed like they were right in front of me, in my face. I knew I was having a bad reaction and the best place for me was to stay sitting on the couch. I remember freaking out when I saw the baby lying beside me."

"Did you do any other drugs that night?"

"Yes, I did. Somewhere between nine o'clock and midnight I snorted approximately six lines of cocaine."

"If you knew you were having a bad reaction to the PCP, why did you do cocaine?"

"I started to come down from the PCP so I figured I'd be fine."

"Did you stay at the house that night?"

"Yes, I did. I slept downstairs in Patty's daughter's bedroom."

"Do you recall what happened the next morning?"

"I remember Doug came in and woke me up around seven o'clock in the morning. He said, 'Get up. There's lots of work to do.' I think I got up and put my clothes on but then lay back down and fell asleep again because then Linda came down and stirred me up. I imagine I was a little grouchy and tired from the night before. I wasn't particularly feeling my best, so I popped about fifteen black capsules of caffeine pills to get me going."

"What happened next?"

"I went upstairs to the kitchen and started making breakfast. The electricity was still out so all I could do was cereal. I made some for Jason, too, because Patty was still sleeping. Before leaving for Boston, Doug gave me a list of chores to do around the farm, including cleaning out the chicken shit. Karen and Peter were still there, but they were getting ready to head out. Before they left, Doug brought me down to the barn to show me some other things he wanted me to do aside from my regular chores. He told me Lester would be coming by later that day to tap some maple trees and to help him if he needed me to. We smoked a joint with Peter before everyone left."

"Did you do the chores Doug left for you?"

"Yeah, and then Patty woke up and started cleaning the house. I finished doing my normal jobs, cleaning the shit out of the chicken coops and putting fresh hay down; cleaning the cow pens out and putting fresh sawdust and hay down for the cows. I stacked the firewood on the front porch and stoked the fire in the woodstove as well as the fireplace in the master bedroom. I was pissed that I had to do all the slave work while everyone else reaped the benefits."

"What benefits?" attorney Roudes asked curiously.

"Bill made all this money and traveled extensively. Doug and Alvin and Peter got the easy jobs and made more money. The women didn't have to do anything except keep the men happy. I was paid crap and did all the shit work. My life sucked and I just didn't care anymore. I knew Bill had thousands of dollars in the master bedroom because I heard Patty telling Karen and Linda about it the night before."

"Did you think you deserved that money?"

"It definitely would have helped me with the predicament I was in. Everything was racing through my head—my probation officer, jail, Cathy. I took some more of the PCP around eleven-thirty that morning and went back to the spot I was sitting on the couch the night before. Jason was sitting on the living room floor playing with some trucks and Patty was cleaning up the house. She was always so happy and confident. I remember seeing her go upstairs to the master bedroom."

"Were you angry with Patty for being happy when your own life was such a mess?"

"No, I liked Patty. She was always good to me."

"Did you follow Patty up to the master bedroom?"

"No. I went into the kitchen and poured a huge glass of vodka."

"If you were so concerned about drinking the night before, why did you drink that morning?"

"I don't know. It was like I couldn't control myself. The next thing I remember was being back in the living room and looking down at Patty crumbled on the floor by the coffee table. I had a butcher knife in my hand. I had stabbed her four times in the back. She looked up at me and said, 'Why, Suds? Why?' I flopped down on the couch and said, 'I don't know why, Patty. I don't know.' Jason came up beside me and started hitting me on the leg with the fire poker. I grabbed it away from him and when I did it must have scraped the side of his face. I thought I had killed him and so I put him in the bathroom. When I went back over to where Patty was, the phone was lying on the floor beside her. When I picked it up, there was a busy signal. I don't know who she tried to call."

"Was Patty dead at that time?"

"No, I don't think so, but from that point on I don't remember anything."

"Did you plan on killing Patricia Keefe on February 26, 1981?"

"I was so distraught over my life that I wanted to numb myself. I took as many drugs as I could to forget about my problems. I was so messed up that I must have blacked out because I don't remember much after that. I don't know why I killed her. I didn't plan to."

"Are you saying the drugs made you kill her?"

"I don't know. But if the devil ever designed a drug it would have been PCP. That stuff is pure evil."

"What is the next thing you remember about that day?"

"I was standing at the top of the spiral staircase and saw Patty's body lying at the bottom. That was when I realized what the f*** I had done."

"What did you realize you had done?"

"There was a massive amount of blood and sections of her internal organs coming out of her abdomen. There was a large gaping hole in her neck, and it looked as though it was cut all the way around. I knew I had to get out of there so I went upstairs and found the bank bag I knew was up there."

"Where did you go from there?"

"I went down to the barn located at the south entrance of the driveway and found the keys to Doug and Linda's Bronco. I drove to Lebanon, where I ditched the car and my clothes. I took a bus to Pennsylvania. I was sitting in a bar when the cops found me."

After Suds' testimony, the State rested. Attorney Roudes' closing arguments summarized most of what I'd already read.

"Preoccupied with his own financial problems and with the loss of his girlfriend, as well as, envious of Bill's apparent success, Steven 'Suds' Sudvari did knowingly and willingly commit murder in the afternoon hours of Thursday, February 26, 1981. We have heard through Patty's friends that they did in fact party the night before, indulging in some drug use, but that it was Suds who repeatedly abused the substances in order to dull the pain and frustration he felt over the stressors in his own life.

"We know that at eleven-thirty that morning the only people left in the house were Patty and her young son Jason, along with Suds. We know that at twelve-thirty, she spoke with her big kids in Massachusetts. We learned in earlier testimony that a Mr. Lester had come by around 2:45 PM to mark some maple trees for sugaring on the property and, although Mr. Lester went up to the house, it appeared to him that no one was home. Mr. Lester stated in his testimony that the Bronco was gone.

"So, between the hours of twelve-thirty and two-thirty the defendant savagely attacked Patricia Keefe with a butcher knife and with a fire poker. He cut her throat and stabbed her repeatedly before throwing her down the basement stairs while her young son tried valiantly to come to his mother's rescue. He was left locked in the bathroom, cold, frightened and alone for over twelve hours before he was rescued by a family friend. You heard graphic testimony from that friend who also discovered Patty's body and the police officer who investigated this case. You also heard expert testimony from Doctor John Dunn who performed the autopsy and provided important evidence in the nature of the attack and extent of Patricia's struggle for her life. How her wrists were shattered from defending herself from repeated blows with the fire poker. That she had over thirty-one stab wounds throughout her upper body.

"Finally, you heard minute details about the defendant's conduct shortly after he committed this grisly crime. That he stole money—over five thousand dollars—which he knew was in the house. That he found the keys to the Bronco that were hidden in the barn and drove to Lebanon, New Hampshire, where he bought new clothes and left his boots in a gas station. After drinking in a bar for a few hours, the defendant took a bus to Pennsylvania, arriving a little more then twenty-four hours after killing Patty, and was found sitting in yet another bar where he was then apprehended. The State submits that there is no question as to who killed Patricia Keefe. The issue is whether the defendant purposely caused her death. Did the defendant, Steven Sudvari, act with premeditation? That is for you to decide based upon the evidence which was presented to you."

It didn't take the jury long to deliberate and find Suds guilty of first degree murder, sentencing him to life in prison without the possibility of parole.

Even after I had finished reading all the testimony, I found myself wanting to know even more about Suds. I still wasn't satisfied and wanted to know why he killed my mother, but that single question had turned into a series of them. Was it genetic? Was he a born killer? Or was it the environment, the circumstance, drugs like he said? Perhaps post-traumatic stress from the Vietnam War as the defense had argued. What was his life like growing up? Was he abused, or did he have parents who loved him? And if he did, how could he have taken my parent away so viciously?

Emotionally drained all I wanted to do at that point was go home and process all the stuff I had just read. Most of it I had already known, just not in detail. The one thing I hadn't known was how long my mother had fought for her life. I couldn't imagine what must have gone through her mind for the two hours she endured such brutality.

Chapter Sixteen

When I returned to school after winter break, I rarely went back to the farm. I threw myself more into the social activities of school than my classes and tried very hard to forget where I came from. But I didn't quite know where I was going, either. I partied my way through the next four months.

It wasn't until the end of my freshman year in college that Bill had to go to court on the gun charges stemming from the bust. The desolate jury box was a reminder that this was a sentencing hearing. Bill had already been found guilty and this was to determine how long he would spend in prison. The prosecution called only one witness—Tony—who testified to the incident that had taken place in the kill room a few years earlier.

In the courtroom, the mahogany benches creaked with the slightest movement as we sat and listened to Tony reluctantly detailing the events of the night in question. As my mind wandered, I recalled all the times he and Sue had spent with James and me. They were wonderful people, the only sane adults in my life, and I hadn't realized how much I missed them until that day.

As Tony left the courtroom, he stopped beside me. With tears in his eyes, he shook his head and said, "I'm sorry. I didn't want to come here today."

I just touched his hand and smiled. I knew that even though he and Bill had their differences, Tony didn't wish anything bad on him. In my crazy world, people felt a certain loyalty for each other—perhaps out of respect or fear that they might someday end up at the bottom of the lake with a pair of cement shoes. Despite Bill's abrasiveness, he exuded an authoritativeness that people were drawn to. Maybe they were just turned on by his obvious abundance of drugs and money. In any event, Bill always had someone watching his back. Unfortunately, those friendships were superficial; once the money and drugs were gone, so were all the people.

Bill was sentenced to nine months in the federal prison at Danbury, Connecticut and had until October 6, 1989 to surrender himself.

During finals week, I realized I needed to make some sort of arrangement for summer, as there was no way in hell I would go back to the farm.

At lunch one day, my friend Christy asked, "What are your plans for summer, Jen?"

"I don't know," I responded with a sigh. "I haven't figured that out yet."

"If you want, you can come home with me to Cape Cod. I'm sure I can get you a waitressing job where I work, and my parents would have no problem with you staying with us."

"Oh my God, that would be awesome!" I said.

"Great! Then it's settled. I'll let my parents know you're coming."

Christy came from a wealthy family and I was really looking forward to my summer on Cape Cod. Unfortunately, it was short-lived; bad things seem to follow me wherever I go.

Having never been to that part of Massachusetts before, I spent my first week getting to know the area and settling into her family's enormous house. I hadn't even started working yet.

On Friday night we decided to go out with her aunt Lisa and a couple of her aunt's male friends. We were having a great time dancing and drinking at a beach bar. I couldn't believe how lucky I was to be spending my summer down there. After only one drink, I started to feel sick and light-headed.

"Are you okay?" one of the guys asked me.

"I don't feel very well," I responded. "It must be from being out in the sun all day. I think I need to lie down."

"Here, let me take you back to Christy's house," he offered politely. "You wait here and I'll let her know."

"Thank you," I said drowsily.

After that, I don't remember anything until I woke up lying on the grass outside Christy's front yard. My white sundress was up over my head and this man I had just met was fumbling with my panties as he forced himself inside me. I frantically looked around for something to hit him with, but there was nothing. I kicked and squirmed, desperately trying to break free, but my body felt weak and numb. *Oh my God, this isn't happening.*

"Get off me!" I screamed. With every bit of strength I had, I managed to push him off.

As I tried to get on my feet, he grabbed me again and pinned me down. "You know you want it, you little bitch," he said. His face was so close to mine I could smell the stench of alcohol on his breath.

My futile attempt to break free left me lying broken on the front lawn of Christy's house. I couldn't comprehend what had just happened to me. I was in shock as I realized that he must have drugged my drink. I picked myself up off the ground and went inside and all I could think about was getting out of there. I waited until the effects wore off and when Christy still wasn't home from the bar by two o'clock in the morning I packed my things, got into my old black Mazda and drove the six hours back to New Hampshire.

When I arrived at the farm early that morning, Bill and Carry weren't even surprised to see me. "That was a quick summer," Bill said sarcastically.

"I'm tired," was all I said as I went down to my room and crashed.

It took me days to process what had happened. I had been raped. Every time Christy called, I told whoever answered to tell her I wasn't home. I didn't blame her, but I also didn't know what to say. After a few weeks of excuses why I couldn't take her call she stopped trying.

The Turkey Farm – Behind the Smile

My relationship with Carry was still strained, but for some reason I felt the need to tell her what had happened. One warm day in June, about three weeks after the incident on Cape Cod, I found myself alone with Carry at the farm. Bill was on his produce run, his only remaining business. My brothers were in their last week of school before summer vacation.

Sitting on her bed in the upstairs master bedroom watching her put clean clothes away, I mustered up the courage to tell her why I had come home. The tears that streamed down my face must have shown her how painful this was for me and how much I was hurting inside. In the eight years she had known me, she had never seen me cry.

"Do you want to know why I came home from the Cape?"

"I'm sure whatever the reason, you invited it," was her only response.

The stone coldness in her tone took my breath away. I hadn't even gotten the words out before she assumed it was something I did. Here I was about to pour my heart out to this woman, who was supposed to be my surrogate mom, and all she could do was twist it around so it was my fault—I had asked for it; I should have known better.

As I left her room that day, my hatred for Carry was sealed.

After James graduated from high school in June, 1989 we moved together to Waterville Valley and shared an apartment. He, too, refused to stay at the farm any longer. Bill still had his produce run, but with no one left on the farm to run the turkey business, and the feds on the verge of foreclosure, it folded. In order to supplement his income he'd taken a job as head cook at a restaurant. As fate would have it, or the curse that continued to follow me, this restaurant was the same one where James and I worked as waiters. There we were again, under his thumb, and he was bossing us around. But this time it was different—we were now living on our own.

That summer was a time of experimentation for me. It was the freest time of my life; I had no responsibilities except working and paying my rent. My best friend Sha had returned from California and we reconnected with some other friends from high school. We were inseparable; we all worked together, lived together and partied together. My friends became family to me.

We were like butterflies emerging from our cocoons, pre-adolescents on our own for the first time. We wanted a summer of fun, a time we could look back on with fondness later when we were married with children. *Summer of '69* by Bryan Adams was our theme song that summer. We spent our days swimming in the lake, tubing down the river and hiking in the mountains, then wait tables at night and, with a fistful of money, party until dawn. Watching the sun come up was invigorating back then. Seeing the sunrise now always reminds me of those carefree days.

I was so happy that Sha was back in town. She became the safety deposit box for all my deep, dark secrets— including the ones I'd tried so desperately to hide during high school. She was the only person that knew I'd gone to the court house and read the transcripts from the murder trial, not even my brother knew. And she supported my desire to someday meet face to face with Suds. Sha would listen as I spewed my hatred toward Bill and Carry and all they'd done to me. Through her I was able to see how life could have been and should have been, but at the same time realized that no one's family is perfect. Sha was to me what Nard was to my mom. She accepted me for who I was and didn't judge me or expect anything from me.

In early October of that year, Bill was scheduled to surrender to the federal prison in Danbury, Connecticut for gun charges stemming from the bust in 1987. As usual, I was the one who drove him. I took Sha with me. By then she knew everything and had been around Bill enough at work, so nothing fazed her about him. We viewed it as just a road trip. Because we had to leave so early in the morning, Sha and I stayed at the farm the night before. While Bill was getting his affairs in order, Carry went to Ames, the local department store, and bought Bill four sets of grey sweat suits, which would be his uniform for the next nine months. Despite the circumstances, Bill was actually in pretty good spirits that night.

The next morning we got up around five o'clock so we could be on the road by six. Bill had to be at the prison by noon, but it was a good four hours away and he wanted to have time to stop for his last real meal. We drove Carry's father's Crown Vic, an old police car equipped with a CB radio (this would later come in handy). It felt strange driving my stepfather to surrender to a federal prison in my step-grandfather's old police car. Bill rolled a few joints for the "road trip" but couldn't smoke them himself. He wanted us to smoke so that when he walked into the prison he'd reek of pot but then pass the piss test. It was just another one of his twisted mind games. Bill thought it would be fun to "f*** with the guards."

As we drove up the private paved road toward the prison, the fields on either side were as green as could be. The grounds were beautifully landscaped, and the modern-looking buildings looked more like offices than a prison. After parking the car in the lower lot, the three of us walked toward the visitors building. I was annoyed at having to listen to Bill dictate all the responsibilities he was dumping on me again while he was in jail, not to mention totally paranoid that I was walking into a federal prison "high" on marijuana.

Bill walked up to the guard sitting behind a Plexiglass partition and said in his loud voice, "Where does one go to surrender?"

Despite how I felt about Bill, that was painful for me to hear. This man, who'd always seemed bigger than life, was surrendering himself to spend the next nine months incarcerated. The sad part about it was that if he had just filed the proper paperwork when he was a teenager, he wouldn't have been in this mess and most likely wouldn't have lost the farm, either.

After the guard had taken Bill away, Sha and I went back to the car.

"I feel so bad for him, Jen," Sha said as she looked back toward the prison.

"Ahh, he'll be fine. He's in Club Fed," I said, stretching my arms out to show the beautifully landscaped compound.

"I know, but it's just so weird leaving him like that. I feel like I could cry."

"You're so good, Sha," I said with a laugh. "But Bill made his choices in life, and this is the consequence. Don't worry he's right in his element. By the end of the day he'll be king of his cell block."

I had no doubt that Sha considered this one of the craziest experiences of her life. And it was about to get better. I was used to stuff like this, but she'd had a relatively sheltered childhood, coming from a traditional All-American family. She still had both her parents and life had been good to her.

After getting lost on our way home and attempting to use the CB radio to call for help, we managed to find our way.

"I feel like we're in a Thelma and Louise movie," Sha said once we were headed in the right direction.

"Hanging out with me is never dull, I'll give you that," I replied.

At that time, James, Sha, our friend Jackie and I were all living in a condo at Waterville Estates in Campton. No longer waitressing and making hundreds of dollars a night, we were poorer than poor. We worked as chambermaids for minimum wage and didn't even have enough money to get the electricity turned on. We cooked on the woodstove and ate by candlelight every night. The only food we had was whatever people had left behind in the hotel rooms we cleaned. They were efficiency rooms for skiers, so sometimes we got some good stuff like chicken and steak left in freezers and unopened boxes of cereal. It really wasn't that bad and we made the best of our hippie-like lifestyle. During that time, James taught himself how to play the guitar and Sha and I amused ourselves by playing marathon card games of Rummy.

Before Bill left on his hiatus at Club Fed, he'd informed James and me that we were to take over his produce run while he was away. Sha also offered to help, so every Wednesday night we would get out of work around three o'clock in the afternoon and drive a U-Hall down to Massachusetts. Bill always had different places lined up for us to stay. At first it was awkward going up to a stranger's door and saying, "We're Bill's kids and he told us we could stay here tonight." But after a while it got easier and we came to enjoy our weekly runs. It was always an adventure, and even got to the point where our friends wanted to tag along.

The produce market opened at 4:00 AM, so we would get up at 3:00 AM, grab a coffee at Dunkin Donuts and head to the market. We'd spend the next couple of hours bargaining for the best deals on lettuce, tomatoes, cucumbers and anything else on our list with men who barely spoke English. It didn't take long to figure out that they'd give Sha and me a better price than they'd give James so he'd wait in the truck while Sha and I went to buy the produce. Then we would drive back to New Hampshire and deliver to the local restaurants.

During one of our runs we stayed at the house of someone whose neighbor had a statue of the Virgin Mary on their lawn. It was November so there was a dusting of snow on the ground. Our friend Donny, who had tagged along that week, decided at three in the morning that he wanted the four-foot statue, so he hopped the fence and grabbed it. We thought it was plastic but it turned out to be ceramic and heavy as hell. It took all four of us to get it over the fence and into the truck. Having parked on a hill, when we pulled away the statue fell over and the head broke off.

"Great, now we're cursed," I said half jokingly.

Once home, we brought the statue into our condo and placed in under the spiral staircase, carefully setting the head back in place. I swear to God, after that we had a streak of bad luck and I was convinced it was because of the statue. First, James fell through a loose step on the staircase and broke his ankle. Then Jackie, our other roommate, accidentally threw $180 cash into the woodstove. It was a refund of the security deposit at the last place she'd rented and we were planning to use the money to turn on the electricity.

Once we got over the shock of the burned money, Jackie said, pointing to Sha and me, "Well, you two are the only ones who haven't had anything bad happen to you yet."

"I'm telling you, it's the curse of the statue," I announced.

Relax Jen," Donny said, "There's no such thing as a curse."

"Yea well, I've had enough bad shit happen to me in my life and I'm not taking any chances. I'm trying to get on God's good side. We need to put that thing back before anything else happens."

A week later Sha and I were on our way to pick up Jackie from work. It was the day before Thanksgiving and it had snowed the night before. The sun was shining brightly that day and when it hit the windshield it was blinding. We drove down the winding dirt road toward town talking about what was happening on our favorite soap, *General Hospital*. The next thing I remember was waking up with my head resting on the steering wheel. My right hand throbbed and I couldn't figure out why we had stopped. I tried to open my eyes but they felt like they were glued shut. When I was finally able to focus, I looked over and saw Sha crumpled in the passenger seat. She wasn't moving. In the distance I could hear a voice saying, "Everything's going to be okay. The ambulance is on its way."

Still not sure what was happening, I looked out the driver's side window and saw my brother standing there. He was white as a ghost as he opened the car door.

"Oh my God, are you okay?" he asked frantically.

"What happened?" I said groggily.

"You've had an accident. I was on my way home and came upon you...oh shit, is she dead?" James asked, looking at Sha.

Just then Sha started to stir and sat up. Her face was one big bloody mess; it looked as if someone had pulled the skin right off. As Sha reached for the visor to look in the mirror, James reached in and flipped it back up.

"Don't look," he said firmly.

Obviously in shock Sha started to shake violently and lost consciousness again.

Meanwhile, when we hadn't shown up, Jackie had hitched a ride home with our boss. News traveled fast about our accident, and by the time we arrived at the hospital Sha's parents and Carry were already there, as were a bunch of our friends. I was released a few hours later, but Sha went into surgery to have glass removed from over 80 percent of her face. James (who was still shaken up) and I went home with Sha's parents and stayed with them for the night.

The next day Sha's mother and I went to the hospital to pick her up. For the first time since my mom had died, I feared I might lose someone very close to me. Even though I knew she was okay, I was afraid she would hate me. To my relief, she wasn't mad at me at all, and we went back to her parents' house for Thanksgiving dinner. That year, we had a lot to be thankful for.

On the way back to our condo that night, Sha's dad explained to us what had happened. Apparently, a commercial-sized wood chipper was parked on the narrow road so workers could cut down some trees. Because the sun had blinded my vision when I came around the S-curve and there were no signs warning motorists about the parked vehicle, I was unaware the chipper was there and hit it head-on. Thankfully, Sha had put her head back and closed her eyes to avoid the bright sunlight. This saved her life. The doctor said that if her body hadn't been like a rag doll when she hit the windshield she would probably have died. Three men had been working that day. The one in the bucket cutting down branches had flown two hundred feet into the woods. One of the other workers ran to the nearest house and called 911. Passing the garage where my car was towed, we stopped to see the damage. My uninsured Mazda was totaled. To my horror, I could see the imprint of Sha's face in the windshield.

After that, we decided to dispose of the statue we'd stolen. We brought it with us on our next produce run so we could return it to its rightful owner. Unable to find the location, James had the brilliant idea of putting it on our mother's grave, so that's what we did.

The next day, Nana called and said, "I went to your mother's grave today, Jennifer. Somebody has put a statue of the Virgin Mary on it." She was clearly annoyed.

I assured Nana that I didn't know anything about it. The next day we drove back down to Massachusetts and went to my mother's grave. After retrieving the statue, we searched until we finally found the owner and put it back where it belonged.

"Now maybe the curse will lift," I said to my friends, still convinced the theft of the statue had been the reason for all our bad luck.

Chapter Seventeen

Even though I hadn't returned to Plymouth State College in the fall I knew I needed to make plans to go back to school. I enjoyed my time off to find myself, but I couldn't continue this way forever. As winter gave way to spring Sha and I began to talk about going to school in Florida, where one of our friends was residing. We both applied and were accepted to Daytona Beach Community College. But just as Sha was preparing to move ahead of me and get things settled, I met the man of my dreams.

My brother James introduced me to Tim at a broomball banquet in May 1990. I was instantly attracted to him and knew my life would never be the same. After meeting him again at a party two weeks later, our fate was sealed, we were inseparable and moved in together a few months later.

My choice to not move to Florida with Sha would vastly change the course of my life.

When I first met Tim, I was still dating Patrick. In high school, Patrick was the guy all the girls wanted to date. At that time, however, girls weren't really on his priority list, and that fascinated me. He was distracted only by things that were important to him: his school studies, sports and family. He was a challenge to me and I was pretty relentless in that pursuit. For the first two years we dated, I was totally in love with him. But then, when I went to Plymouth State College, I realized there was a whole other world out there and I wanted a piece of it. Patrick went off to college in Manchester, New Hampshire, more than an hour away and we rarely saw one another.

Patrick and I continued to date on and off during my first year of college and the following year when I didn't return to college. But if I had an opportunity to go out with someone else, I did. I figured what he didn't know wouldn't hurt him. The examples I had growing up regarding relationships did not teach me the morals and respect I should have shown Patrick, so I cheated on him repeatedly, never once feeling guilty or ashamed. I guess you could say I wanted to "have my cake and eat it, too."

When I met Tim, however, everything changed. I thought I'd found my soul mate; he was an experienced man, much older, with dreams and ambitions that excited me. Patrick was still just a boy who wanted a simple life like his parents. But my life had never been simple and probably never would be. The thought of staying with Patrick suddenly made me feel claustrophobic and tied down.

On the night I decided to break up with Patrick (Years later, this would cause me a great deal of pain.) we stood in the kitchen of my rented apartment and I said, "I need space right now, Patrick. I can't see you anymore."

"Is it another guy?" he asked, torn between anger and hurt.

"No, no, no," I assured him, lying through my teeth. All I could think about was how infatuated I was with Tim and how much I wanted to spend every waking moment with him.

"I am never gonna love anyone else as much as I love you right now," he said as tears welled up in his eyes.

After four years together, his words didn't faze me. Not even his fervent display of emotion touched me. I stood there, numb, waiting for him to leave. Lying came naturally to me in those days, and I felt no remorse for breaking Patrick's heart.

In hindsight, I feel very guilty about how I treated him. It has made me feel sad over the years. The crazy thing of it is that I really did love Patrick. He was good to me, sticking by me through some very difficult times. He came from a good family and he was ambitious, going to college to become an X-ray Technician. Deep down inside, I knew he would make a good husband and father. But for some reason that wasn't enough. Back then, I was in search of something else. What exactly that was, I didn't know.

My relationship with Tim moved quickly. We began dating in May 1990 and by August were living together. In the beginning Tim was everything I had hoped for. He had a Trans Am and a truck, he owned his own business and, being six years older than I (he was twenty-five and I was nineteen), he seemed very mature. Tim had also been married before, and I naively figured he must have learned something from the mistakes of his first marriage and would be a better husband the second time around. I had spent the past two years finding myself but was ready for something more, something real. Like most little girls, I dreamed of meeting my prince charming and living happily ever after in a little house with a white picket fence. Given my difficult childhood, I figured God would make that happen. I'd paid my dues and deserved a better life.

Tim and I discussed marriage early on in our relationship. We swore we would be together forever. That alone was a huge attraction for me; all I wanted for my future was stability. What appealed to me most were the great conversations we had about life and our upbringing, most importantly how our life would never be like our parents'. He, too, had come from a divorced and very dysfunctional family, and we shared stories about how our parents' choices had affected us growing up. He insisted he would never bring up his own children that way.

I shared with Tim things about my past that I hadn't shared with many people (except Sha), particularly men. For the first time in my life, I felt that to be in a healthy relationship I had to be honest about things that had happened in my past and how they made me feel, something I'd never thought was important in my relationship with Patrick. Back then I thought some things were better left unsaid. I was certain that being truthful with Tim regarding the things I'd been accustomed to lying about my whole life would give us a solid foundation for the future.

As I shared the stories of my childhood—my mother's death, the people I grew up with, the bust and the drugs—he was very compassionate and understanding. He held me while I poured out my deepest, darkest secrets to him, and for the first time in my life I felt safe and protected. Even when I told him that smoking marijuana occasionally was just a part of who I was, he understood. I assured him that I didn't abuse it or smoke it all the time; it was something I had grown accustomed to and enjoyed at the end of the day.

"It's part of my genetic makeup," I teased.

"Everyone has their vice" he responded.

Tim was very supportive when I told him that I'd attempted to meet with the man responsible for my mother's death and still had a strong need to do so. I explained to him how Bill had put an end to that meeting before it had occurred. He encouraged me to pursue it if it meant I'd find closure. I felt a tremendous sense of relief being open with Tim and was sure we were starting out on the right foot. Like most people, he never liked Bill and often said, "Why don't you just get away from him? He's evil." For the sake of my relationship with Tim, I did distance myself from Bill for a while.

Even though I had backed out of going to Florida with Sha (she hated it and come home after six weeks) I still intended to go back to school. I wanted to follow in my mother's footsteps and go to nursing school. When I began talking about going back to school, Tim supported my decision and offered to help me in any way he could. In September 1990, I enrolled at LaBour Nursing School in Dorchester, Massachusetts just outside South Boston. During the week, I lived in the dorm and came home to Tim on the weekends. Within a month, however, I found out I was pregnant. Being at an all-girls catholic school, I was forced to hide my pregnancy for fear I would be kicked out.

My Nana didn't live very far from the school so I made an effort to see her as often as I could; as often as she saw me over the years anyway. Being a devote catholic, she wasn't very happy with me when she learned I was living with a man out of wedlock, so I couldn't imagine how she would react when she found out I was pregnant. Our relationship was strained because I harbored a lot of resentment toward her and my auntie. When it came to my feelings of abandonment, I sort of lumped them together because neither one of them had ever attempted to take my brothers and me away from the farm after our mother's death. I felt unworthy of their love and affection; otherwise, they would surely have taken us in.

Being a tiny person, I didn't show for some time, but when I was about six months pregnant my baggy clothes started to fill out.

"Are you gaining weight, Jennifer?" Nana asked one afternoon when she stopped by the school to take me to lunch.

"Yeah. You know how it is at college, Nan. You eat junk on the run and the pounds creep up. I'll lose it come summer," I assured her and then quickly changed the subject. "So, how is Auntie?" I asked more out of obligation than real interest.

"She and Uncle Fred are busy making plans to remodel the downstairs and add on to the house," she answered happily.

"Are they planning on living with you forever?" I snapped.

"Now, Jennifer," she said derisively, "you know that your aunt and uncle have been a tremendous help to your grandfather and me over the years. You don't have to be so snide."

Auntie, her husband and their kids had lived with Nana for years—since they'd been married, in fact. This only added salt to my wounds. They both had good jobs and could comfortably afford to live on their own, but instead it appeared they were taking advantage of my Nana. If *they* could live with her all this time, then why couldn't Nana have taken in three motherless little kids?

"Nobody likes an unhappy person," Nana said. That was her way of changing the subject.

So, I put on my happy face and acted like everything was fine. I shoved all the painful feelings and frustrations deeper within me. It was easier that way. I only hoped that some day I would do something that would make Nana proud of me and worthy of her love.

After lunch we returned to my school. As we stood on the sidewalk outside the dorm Nana said, "You really should do something about that weight you've gained, Jennifer. It's not very flattering on you."

With that she gave me a hug and then she slid behind the wheel of her car and drove away.

"Thanks, Nan," I mumbled to myself as I turned and walked into the historic brick building.

I was able to successfully finish my first year of nursing school without incident. But I knew it was time to come clean with Nana and tell her about my pregnancy. I secretly prayed that after she was finished being angry and disappointed, she'd be proud of the fact that I was giving her her first great-grandchild.

"Oh, Jennifer!" Nana cried over the phone when I called to tell her. "How could you let this happen?"

"I know you're upset with me," I responded confidently, "but I'm very happy about becoming a mother and I hope you can be happy for me."

"What are you going to do about school? You can't very well go back in the fall with a new baby."

"I'm going to take a year off and transfer my credits to New Hampshire and then go back and finish." I was positive things would turn out the way I'd planned.

"Well, I guess there's nothing you can do about it now," she replied ruefully. "I just wish you had been more responsible with yourself. This is probably a result of what those people taught you living at that place."

I could feel my blood start to boil. I wanted to scream, *You're the one who let me live with "those people at that place!"* While I was relieved that everything was now out in the open. I fumed at her implication that the farm was the reason for my problems when she could have done something about it.

Chapter Eighteen

My daughter Katelyn was born at 5:05 PM on a warm June day in 1991. She weighed 7 pounds, 11 ounces and was 20½ inches long. She was a perfect looking baby, all pink with no wrinkles or rashes like most newborns. Katelyn entered the world with her eyes wide open, looking around inquisitively. The moment they placed that little bundle in my arm, it struck me that I was now a mom. This was a mixed blessing because it also made me miss my own mother. I wondered if this was how she felt when I was born.

It took me a couple of days to bond with Katelyn, but I vividly recall when I finally did. I had gone to the market to get diapers and formula and when I returned home I walked into the living room. Katelyn was lying on Tim's chest and they were napping together on the couch. It was at that moment that I realized that I loved that child as I had never loved before.

Motherhood caused me to become aware of many things. I realized I functioned in the subconscious. My maternal instincts were so strong that even when I didn't believe I would know what to do, something inside me did know. In spite of only a brief example with my mom, parenting came naturally. As with most people, having a child made me see the world in a different light. Things that were once important didn't seem so important anymore. Having gone through a few years of being a selfish, carefree teenager, I suddenly found myself responsible for someone else and had to put my daughter's needs before mine. I did so willingly. Being a mom was a dream come true and filled the gaping hole I didn't realize was in my heart.

It was like a rebirth. The emotional wall I'd created to protect me all those years didn't stand a chance against the powerful love I felt for my child.

A year later, after careful soul searching—and I was sure I knew the good and the bad components of Tim's personality—I made the choice to marry him. My wedding day was another dream-come-true for me, and I felt like Cinderella. My mother believed in reincarnation and the afterlife, so I always thought she would appear on the most monumental day of my life, my wedding. Sitting on the edge of the queen-sized bed, I waited for a sign.

"Okay, Mom, if you're coming now is the time," I said aloud when I found myself alone in the hotel room. "Everyone is gone. Today is a very special day for me and I know you can't let it continue without giving me your blessing."

While sitting patiently for her to appear, it never occurred to me that she wouldn't. At one point I got up off the bed and started walking toward the door. "Last chance," I said. "I'm leaving for the church now."

Just then the door opened and Sha popped her head in. "Who are you talking to, Jen?" she asked.

"No one," I responded, a little embarrassed as I snapped back to reality.

"Well, let's go," she continued. "The limo is here and there are tequila shots waiting for you in the bar."

My mom never did appear that day. For a brief moment, disappointment washed over me. Looking back, I can't help but wonder if she didn't show because she knew what a jerk Tim would turn out to be.

My wedding was very traditional. We had an enormous Catholic wedding with my brother James walking me down the isle. Even though Bill had raised me, he wasn't my real dad. My real dad was a drunk, and I didn't have much of a relationship with him. I chose James because I felt he represented everything the person in that role should. We'd been through so much together I thought it fitting that he should give me away.

For the traditional father/daughter dance, I chose the song *Wind Beneath my Wings* by Bette Midler. The words to that song perfectly described my feelings about my relationship with James. I explained to the DJ that I would be dancing to that song with my brother, *not* my father. But when it came time for the dance, the DJ said, "Will the father of the bride please meet her on the dance floor." The room was uncomfortably silent when both Bill and my real dad stood up and started walking toward me. I looked at James in desperation, hoping he would come to my rescue, knowing it was supposed to be him. But before I knew it, Bill had sat back down and my dad had staggered to the center of the dance floor, wrapped his arms around my waist, and nestled his face in the side of my neck. Tears of disappointment welled in my eyes as I made the best of the situation.

As a wife and mother, I believe I gave 110 percent, to the point that I felt I had lost myself. I was consumed with making sure I didn't disappoint Tim or bear any resemblance to his first wife. But once the honeymoon period was over Tim's true colors were revealed. By the time I became pregnant with our second child our marriage was already falling apart. Tim's dream to be a famous race car driver took precedence over everything else, including his family. He was either at work or at the garage working on his race car, while I was holed up at home nine months pregnant with a two-year-old. Tim moved us an hour away from everyone I knew to a little town called Tufftonborough. We lived in a rented house nestled in the woods miles from civilization with no phone or cable, and I drove a car that was slowly falling apart. Unable to see the long-term effects of the choice I'd made, I lived only for the moment, believing love would get me through. I figured if I loved Tim enough, kept the house clean enough and took care of our daughter well enough while keeping a happy smile on my face, he would eventually see what is important.

But loneliness and despair slowly consumed me and I felt isolated from my family and friends. I was twenty-two years old and still living in a fantasy world. Something inside me secretly hoped that if we had a boy Tim would change and become the man I thought he was when I married him. His constant comment, "If that's not a boy in there, you're gonna look like this again next year," had me praying every day for a boy. At that point I couldn't imagine another minute with Tim, let alone having another kid with him. As it was, I was already feeling like a single married woman.

On a warm October day in 1993 I was shopping in Laconia with Sha when I went into labor. We rushed to the hospital, Katelyn in toe. Tim was at the Loudon Race Track about forty-five minutes away. Sha called the track from the payphone down the hall and had Tim paged.

"What did he say?" I asked through clenched teeth as another contraction began.

"He said, 'great timing' and then slammed down the phone."

Tim made it just in time for Jaran's arrival. He entered the room saying, "This better be a boy" then flipped on the television set and started watching the race. While I screamed and pushed, exhausted from the pain, Tim and the doctor chatted about who was winning the race.

Jaran was born at 2:52 PM. He weighed 7 pounds, 11 ounces and was 19 3/4 inches long. Unlike Katelyn, he was very hairy and wrinkly. He looked like a 90-year old man.

"Good job," Tim said as he bent down a kissed me on the forehead. Then he walked out the door and went back to the racetrack.

It was then that I really began to hate him.

My worst day ever came only a week later. It was an unseasonably warm day and I had to be in court at 1:30 PM for an unpaid veterinarian bill. (It was actually for Tim's dog but because I was the one who'd brought it to the vet, the bill was in my name.) Katelyn had been sick for a day or two and had woken up that morning with sores in her mouth. They were unlike anything I had seen before. Since I didn't have a phone, I packed up the kids (Jaran was only six days old) and drove to Sha's house where I called the pediatrician's office. The only appointment they could give me was at the same time I had to be in court. Desperate, I took the appointment. I figured I would call the court and explain that my daughter's health was more important. Surly they'd understand.

"Hello. My name is Jennifer and I am supposed to be in court at one-thirty this afternoon but my daughter is very sick and the only appointment I could get was for the same time. Is there any way I can reschedule my hearing until later?"

"Nope," the lady on the other end said coldly. "If you're not here at your scheduled time, a bench warrant will be issued for your arrest."

"Excuse me?" I replied in shock.

"If you are not here for your hearing, you will be arrested," she repeated.

"Well then, I guess you'll just have to arrest me because my daughter is sick and I have to take her to the doctor," I snapped.

"Very well," she replied. The dial tone let me know the conversation was over.

I couldn't believe that I could be arrested for something as trivial as an unpaid vet bill, or that my daughter's wellbeing wasn't enough to excuse me from my hearing until another time. I felt like a criminal. My day had only just begun and I couldn't wait to get home.

At the pediatrician's office the doctor walked in, took one look at Katelyn and said, "She has herpes."

"What!" I responded, mortified.

"It sounds worse than it is," he explained. "Herpes in children is just a form of fever blisters, not a sexually transmitted disease. Once they break, she'll be fine."

"Is there anything I can give her?" I asked.

"Some Tylenol for the pain and fever, and make sure she doesn't get dehydrated. Popsicles would feel good in her mouth."

Still stunned that my daughter had herpes, we left the doctor's office and made our way back to the car. Seeing our black lab in the backseat reminded me of my missed court appointment. I realized I could be arrested at any moment and wondered when and where it would happen. Jaran began to cry. As I took hold of Katelyn's hand I could see just how tired and worn out she was.

"Hey, pumpkin, we just have to stop at the store and then we'll go home so you can lie down."

Pulling into the Hatch Plaza parking lot, I grabbed Jaran, who was still in his infant seat, and unbuckled Katelyn from her car seat. We ran over to the supermarket so I could pick up a few groceries and ice pops for Katelyn and then next door to Ames' Department store.

"We just have to run in and get Jaran a bouncy seat," I said to Katelyn as we headed toward the department store.

Before I even reached the baby section, Katelyn let out a bloodcurdling scream. Startled, I turned around. All I could see was blood gushing from her mouth. The blisters had popped. Katelyn's wails had started Jaran crying, and everyone in the store seemed to be staring at me. I could only imagine what they must have been thinking. Horrified, I bent down and picked Katelyn up with my free arm and scrambled out of the store.

I took a spit-up rag from Jaran's diaper bag and cleaned Katelyn up the best I could. Our ride home was at least an hour. I knew that all she needed was some medicine and a nap to help her feel better. And frankly, I needed to sit on my couch and "relax." On days like that, I depended on my little "vice" to get me through. At that point my nerves were shot. I couldn't imagine what else could possibly go wrong that day.

Driving down Route 3 around Squam Lake in Holderness (Where the movie On Golden Pond was filmed), the foliage was blazing with the fiery colors New Hampshire is so famous for. Both the kids had fallen asleep and the quiet allowed me some peace to process my day so far. Suddenly, my car started to sputter and stall. Thankfully, it was right in front of an auto mechanic's garage. Sitting in the car, I waited for someone to come over and help me, but no one did. The kids were still sleeping so I got out of the car and walked into one of the bays. There must have been six guys in there, but nobody even looked at me. I walked back out and checked on the kids. The sun was beating in through the window and the dog had positioned himself over the passenger seat. Hot and thirsty, he was salivating all over Katelyn's curly blond hair, which was now wet and plastered to her head. Jaran started to squirm and I knew he was probably hungry. My milk-filled breasts told me it was way past feeding time.

Frustrated and not knowing what to do, I turned back toward the garage. That's when I saw the sign: "All visitors report to the office." *That's why they've ignored me.* Realizing the mechanics hadn't paid any attention to me because I was in the wrong area I entered the office. Immediately all six guys came from the bay and asked me if I needed help.

"Something's wrong with my car," I said.

The mechanic lifted the hood and after a quick check said, "You're f*****. No oil. You've blown the engine."

"Great. Can I use your phone to call my husband?" I asked, desperately trying to hold back my tears and wondering what else could possibly go wrong.

"Sure, it's right inside," he said, slamming the hood down, which startled the kids and woke them up.

The first time I called Tim's work the secretary answered but disconnected me when she tried to transfer the call to his shop. I called back two more times. Each time she disconnected me. On the third try I firmly explained to her how important it was that I speak to Tim. After a few more attempts, he finally got on the phone. Just as I was about to explain that my car had broken down and I needed a ride, one of the mechanics in the garage revved up the engine to an old race car. Not only was I unable to hear Tim but Katelyn and Jaran both started to scream. I slammed down the phone in frustration and took the kids outside to calm them down before calling Tim again.

"Tim, my car broke down and I need you to come get the kids and me in Holderness."

"What the hell, Jen! I'm right in the middle of something," he said, annoyed that I was interrupting his day.

"My engine is blown. There's nothing I can do right now," I pleaded. "I have the kids, the dog and groceries. Tim, please come and get us so we can go home. Katelyn doesn't feel well."

"I'll be there when I can," he said before slamming the phone down.

I went back to the car and waited at least forty-five minutes. Finally Tim showed up in a little red pickup truck with one bench seat. Somehow I managed to squeeze us all in and then had to listen to Tim bitch about what a horrible day he was having and how I'd just made it worse because now he would have to work late to finish his project. *Blah, blah, blah.*

Oh, you don't even know what a bad day is, Mister, I thought.

After dropping him off at Integrated Water in Moultonboro where he worked, I headed home, thankful it was only fifteen minutes away. At that point all I wanted to do was get the kids settled and sit on the couch for a quiet and relaxing few hours. Without cable I'd become an avid reader and was in the middle of a good Danielle Steele book.

As I pulled into the dirt, tree-lined driveway, I noticed a yellow piece of paper tacked to the front door. Figuring it was a delivery notice or something, I didn't think much of it. Gathering the kids from the car, I walked to the front door and saw that it was an eviction notice. What a perfectly horrific ending to my perfectly horrific day.

"Perfect!" I screamed.

That was the beginning of the end for Tim and me, and the start of my attempt to take back my life. Based on what I had seen growing up, my perception of relationships was a bit jaded. My view was that most relationships were based on secrets and lies and self-indulgence. Now he wasn't even paying the bills. Where was all his money going? My trust in him disintegrated that day. I knew he couldn't give me the life I needed or wanted. The irony of how similar my life had become to that of my mother's wasn't lost on me.

By the grace of God I was able to rent a three-bedroom apartment back in civilization. I borrowed money from Bill for a security deposit (without letting Tim know). When we moved to our new place in November, I gave Tim an ultimatum—either he put time, attention and effort into the kids and me, or he could leave. Surprisingly, he did change a little and for the next couple of months made an extra effort to be home more. He even took us with him when he went to the garage to work on his race car. We began to feel like a real family, and as I began to let my guard down I felt myself falling in love with him again.

In late February Tim asked if he could go to Florida with the guys to work in the pit crew on a nationally televised race and I agreed. It was an opportunity of a lifetime for him, and I knew that if I stopped him he would resent me for it. I wanted to be supportive of his dream, even though I thought it was unrealistic. Tim assured me that he would be gone for only four days, Thursday to Monday.

My hope for an improved marriage was short-lived. When Tim didn't return home on Monday night as planned, I started to worry. A friend of mine, whose boyfriend had also gone with Tim, told me that he'd brought some sleazy girl with him. I'd never even suspected that Tim was cheating on me, especially after I'd given him two beautiful children. I felt like I'd been punched in the stomach. And when she told me that her boyfriend and the rest of the crew that had gone to Florida had already returned home, I thought I would be sick. Tim hadn't even called me.

As I stayed up late that night waiting for him to come home, all kinds of thoughts ran through my head. I realized that his obsession with racing had taken him away for hours and days at a time, giving him ample opportunity to cheat on me, but I still didn't want to believe that he would do this to me. When the phone rang, I looked at the clock. It was almost midnight. I knew it would be Tim.

"Hey, baby," he yelled into the phone. "We had a couple of problems with the race car and I'm going to have to stay down here for a few more days."

I could hear a lot of commotion in the background. When I asked about it, he said he and the guys were out having a beer.

"What's the phone number to the hotel?" I asked numbly because now I knew he was lying. He obviously didn't realize I knew the other guys had come back. "Just in case there's an emergency and I need to get a hold of you."

"I don't know off the top of my head. I'll call you back and let you know. I gotta go," he said hurriedly before hanging up.

The next day I called the girl whose boyfriend had gone down to Florida with Tim and asked her if she could get me the name and phone number of the hotel. When I called, I made sure it was late and that Tim would be sleeping. The phone rang four or five times before finally I heard somebody fumbling with the receiver.

"Hello," a woman said groggily.

"Can I speak to Tim, please?" I asked ever so nicely.

The long silence followed by a dial tone told me everything I needed to know. When Tim returned home a few days later, I greeted him at the door with all his stuff in garbage bags.

"Get out of this house and out of my life right now," I said firmly.

Without saying a word, he picked up the bags put them in his truck and drove away. No argument, no explanation, no apology. Tim left me with a four-month-old colicky baby and a two-and-a-half-year-old and never looked back.

Chapter Nineteen

It wasn't until later that night when my brother James called that I realized the date: February 26th, the anniversary of our mother's death. We never spoke about her and didn't verbally acknowledge the day, but there was comfort in the tradition of calling each other on that particular day. This time it was bittersweet, and it was about to get worse. When I told James that I had kicked Tim out because he was having an affair, he nonchalantly informed me that Tim had cheated on me with a friend of mine before we were married.

"At the time I thought it was the best decision, Jen," he'd explained. "You two had a child together, you were about to get married and I figured some things are better left unsaid. No good would have come out of telling you."

The pain I felt that night when I went to bed was like a knife slicing through my heart. The trust that was broken, the betrayal, was more then I could bear. The ache in my heart was so deep it seemed to reach my soul. I had freely given all of myself to Tim and he'd twisted and hurt me in a way I'd never been hurt before. Adding salt to the wound was my beloved brother's betrayal. James was the one and only person I had left in the whole world. How could he not tell me the man I was about to marry was cheating on me?

I lay in bed unable to sleep, more devastated by my brother keeping such important information from me than by Tim's infidelity, even though a part of me understood his reason for not telling me. Could I ever trust another soul as long as I lived? It would take years for me to get past my brother's betrayal.

My relationship with James was greatly affected by this and we grew distant. Through everything we'd experienced in life he had always been my rock. If he could lie to me about this, what else had he lied to me about? I think the fact that it all happened at once—the two men I cherished the most hurting me so deeply—magnified my feelings. I shut down emotionally again. I felt more alone than ever.

Somehow I made it through the next few months with no job and no money. Tim hardly saw the kids. I took a Certified Nurses Assistant position at a nursing home in Meredith during the day and worked as a waitress at The Jack O'Lantern, a golf resort in Woodstock, on the weekends. Even after I started working, Tim rarely took the kids, forcing me to scrounge for a babysitter, ask friends or hire someone I couldn't afford. I was barely making ends meet but held out hope that things would improve.

I should have known if something bad could happen to me it would. Every fear I've ever had has come true: my mom's death, the bust, a broken marriage. Life just seems to inflict hardship on me at every turn. I am a good person, yet I can't seem to get a break to save my soul. I've always had a feeling deep inside that I was destined to do something good in life. But I keep finding myself in situations that contradict that and force me to wonder if I'm not just on this earth to suffer. Every time my life starts on the uphill, something forces me back down.

Occasionally I had what I called "sympathy sex" with Tim. I justified it to myself by thinking if I was giving it to him he wouldn't be looking for it somewhere else. But if it didn't stop him while we were married (and apparently before), what made me think it would after we separated? I guess a part of me still held out hope that my marriage would work out. I wanted to believe that after everything I had endured in my life, God would bless me with a "happily ever after."

Six months after Tim and I separated, I found out I was pregnant again. It was like a death sentence. That was the day I hit rock bottom, and for a moment death seemed better than living. The load was too heavy to carry any longer. How could I have a third child with a man I couldn't trust or depend on? I knew I had to tell him and, as pathetic as it sounds, I think I even imagined it would snap Tim into reality.

As I walked up to the door of Tim's condo, I could see through the front window into the living room. I was not prepared for what I saw and I think my heart even stopped. Tim was on the couch having sex with some chick (not the same one he had taken to Florida). Sick to my stomach, I knocked on the door anyway. Turning to check on Katelyn and Jaran who were safely in the car, I took a deep breath.

"We need to talk," I told him when he answered the door, his blond hair messy like he'd just rolled out of bed (which he had, so to speak).

"What's up?" he said, annoyed, as he stepped onto the porch and shut the door behind him.

"I've already seen the tramp inside, Tim," I spat. "You don't need to hide her."

The whole scenario suddenly seemed dirty and shameful. Here I was, his wife, standing on the porch in secret to tell him I was pregnant with his child.

"It's not mine, you slut," he sneered after I told him. "You probably don't even know whose kid it is. Don't think you're going to pin this on me."

Reaching into his pocket, he pulled out a wad of bills and threw them at me. "Here, go take care of it," he said before going back inside.

I couldn't have been in a worse position. Alone raising two babies and pregnant again. I had no money, was behind on my rent, and literally had no one and nowhere to turn. The few friends I had were starting their own families. I couldn't keep turning to them. I knew there was no feasible way I could bring another child into this world, my world, to suffer. It was all I could do to raise the two I had. But the thought of giving the baby away and then knowing I had a child out there somewhere was not something I could handle, either. So I made the only choice I thought I had. It's not something I'm proud of, but with nowhere else to turn, I thought abortion was my only option. That situation took away another little piece of my soul.

After that it seemed to me that it was one thing after another with no end in sight. And just when I thought Tim couldn't get worse, he proved me wrong. Tim seemed to dedicate his life to making mine a living hell, my past being his biggest ammunition. Whenever Tim wanted to make me feel worthless, he'd say something like, "No one will ever want you. You're nothing but a druggie raised by nothing but druggies" or "You asked for everything you got growing up. If you hated Bill so much, you could have left."

I had given all of myself to this man who I believed and trusted, only to be used, abused and thrown away. How could I have been so wrong? After that, I trusted no one, not even myself. What little life remaining in me died and I couldn't see any way out, except death. As I sat, numb, on my bedroom floor one day, I began to wonder if all the horrible things Tim had said to me were true. The kids were down for a nap and I felt as though I were suffocating. Darkness rolled in and consumed me as I began imagining how I would kill myself.

For over three hours I just sat, not just crying but bawling, trying to muster up the courage to take my own life. But then I realized I couldn't leave my kids without a mother, I knew all too well how painfully hard that is. So I decided I would have to take them with me. I couldn't believe I was thinking about such unimaginable things. Suddenly something inside me snapped and a voice said, "Oh, my God, pull yourself together. What are you thinking?"

I know my mother was my guardian angel that day. I believe it was she who rescued me from my despair. After that day, my darkest ever, I vowed not to let Tim, anyone or anything beat me down ever again. I made a promise to myself that when life seemed overwhelming and I hit hard times, when things became so devastating that they consumed my entire world, I would think of how close I had come to giving up and then wait a day.

Right after that I filed for divorce, which was quick and painless because Tim didn't contest a thing. I received all the bills because they were in my name, got full custody of the kids, (God forbid Tim should take responsibility; being a father was an inconvenience to him) and a measly fifty dollars a week in child support.

Success is the best form of revenge and that became my fuel. After I decided to pull my life together, I decided it was also time to finish nursing school.

"You'll never finish," Tim said when I informed him of my plan and that he would have to take more responsibility for his children.

This only motivated me more. I believe Tim expected me to crumble, but I found the strength within to do what was necessary to make a better life for my children and me. That was my focus and I did whatever it took to achieve it.

It was during this time that I began to see the similarities between my life and that of my mother's. I was a young, divorced, single woman raising two young children and trying to finish nursing school, just like her. Honestly the thought scared me a little and I couldn't help but wonder if I'd also find the same horrific fate as her.

Growing up, I had viewed my mom as a victim. After I had kids of my own and could relate to her on a woman-to-woman basis, I began to see her more as a martyr. She had made the ultimate sacrifice for her children in order to provide them with a better life, or so she thought. I realized that she had done what she felt was right at the time, and I certainly couldn't judge her for that. However, I could learn from her mistakes.

Upon that revelation I put a ring on my finger as a symbolic gesture of the promises I'd made to myself—that I would never rely on a man to provide for me and my children; that Katelyn and Jaran were the only relationships I needed in my life and that my devotion was to them and them alone; and that no matter how difficult life got, I would never take the easy way out.

Chapter Twenty

At that time, Jaran was about ten months old. During the day, I was working full-time at a nursing home for $6.50 an hour and waitressing on weekends at "The Jack." My classes were held in Laconia at night. According to our divorce papers, Tim was ordered to take the kids on Wednesday night and every other weekend. One night I went to drop them off at his condo so I could go to school. When he opened the door he said, "I have plans. I can't watch them tonight," and slammed the door in my face.

Furious, my adrenalin kicked into high gear and with Jaran still in my arms I kicked the door open so hard it came right off its hinges. I walked into the kitchen, handed Tim the baby, put the diaper bag on the table, kissed Katelyn on the top of her head and said, "I'll be back to pick them up after class." Then I turned and walked out the door. Tim's jaw was still on the floor when I left.

It was difficult to bring myself to go on welfare, but when I started nursing school in the fall of 1995 I went to the state for daycare assistance. I also automatically qualified for Medicare and food stamps. When these showed up in my mailbox, I was mortified. Putting my pride aside I decided I would accept the help long enough to finish school. But because I opted to work two jobs while going to school, the state took my benefits away after six months.

"It's the only way I can survive," I pleaded with the state agent assigned to my case. "My ex only pays me fifty dollars a week and I have to pay rent, utilities, daycare, groceries—"

"If you go to part-time or quit working all together, you will qualify for all our programs, including tuition for school," she interrupted.

"Are you telling me that if I'm willing to work and go to school to better my life you won't help me, but if I'm willing to live off the state, you will? Something just doesn't seem right here," I responded in disgust.

"That's the way the system works," she said with a shrug.

"Well, there's something seriously wrong with the system," I said as I got up to leave. "Thanks anyway. I'll work three jobs and take out student loans if I have to, but I refuse to take a free ride."

And that is exactly what I did. I picked up another waitressing job and took out more student loans to help with my daily expenses. But it still wasn't enough. It seemed I was always a day late and a dollar short. I found myself looking back on some of the choices my mother had made once she'd found herself alone raising two children. I believe that some of her choices — especially her decision to stay with Bill—were because of her struggle as a single parent. Once she had money and security, it was difficult for her to go back to living on welfare. I vowed not to make the same mistake my mother made.

My greatest fear as a single parent was that my children would be taken away from me. This fear ruled me to the point where I'd make extra sure they were clean and well dressed. I was afraid of what people might think. Unfortunately, we live in a world full of judgment and are defined by how we appear and where we come from. I'd experienced that my whole life and Tim reminded me of it almost daily.

Wanting to ensure that my kids always felt loved, safe and secure, I made sure that at the beginning of the each day I told my children where I would be and what time I'd be back to pick them up. "My job is to go to work and help sick people, and your job is to go to daycare and be good," I would tell them. I believed that my kids needed consistency in their lives and someone who did what she said she would do. I wanted them to know that no matter what the day held for them, at the end of it they would be tucked safely into their own beds. Communication was important to me.

Then the day came when my fear came true (I guess you really do attract what you fear). A man in a dark blue suit showed up at my door and said, "My name is Mr. Brown. I am from Social Services. May I come in?"

He informed me that a complaint had been filed, claiming my children were being neglected and living in filth. I knew immediately that Tim was behind it. I was sickened that he would stoop so low to destroy me. I wanted to scream and tell this man who searched my cupboards and bedrooms that their father hardly ever saw them so he didn't even know what they looked like or how they lived. But I just stood in utter disbelief until Mr. Brown was finished with his investigation.

After asking me a few questions, he seemed satisfied with what he saw and left.

Later that night the phone rang, "Social Services called me and said they were very unhappy with what they found," Tim said.

"You know, Tim, it's disgusting the lengths you will go to make my life hell," I calmly responded. "The only ones you are hurting are the kids."

There was no way I'd let him get a rise out of me. But when I hung up the phone I was shaking so badly I thought I'd pass out. Anxiety wrapped its hands around my throat and I couldn't breath, as my mind raced with panic. Frightened beyond comprehension at the thought of having my children taken away, I couldn't sleep. The next morning, determined to resolve this mess of lies, I called Mr. Brown at Social Services.

"Ms. Keefe, I assure you that I didn't find anything wrong with the way you are raising your children. The case has been closed."

"I'm sorry to have bothered you," I said with relief. "It's just that Tim called me last night and told me you spoke with him and were very unhappy and would be returning."

"I have cases where children are being beaten and neglected in ways you couldn't imagine," Mr. Brown replied. "I don't take kindly to false accusations such as your ex-husband has made."

"Yes I know, and I am very sorry he wasted your time." I couldn't believe I was apologizing for Tim.

"I hope you know that this false report will be included in your file with family court. If you need me to back it up in the future, I would be glad to appear in court on your behalf."

"Thank you, Mr. Brown," I replied. "I appreciate it but hope it never comes to that."

After the incident with Social Services, Tim called them again, claiming that our daughter Katelyn was being molested at daycare and that I knew about it but was doing nothing to stop it. My five-year-old was forced to be examined by the pediatrician, only to confirm it was another false accusation. For me, it was the final straw and nothing after that fazed me. I did whatever it took to protect my children from their father's sick, twisted ways. Unfortunately, I was at the mercy of "the system," and my hands were tied. The courts refused to see what Tim was doing to our children and I had no choice but to continue sending Katelyn and Jaran with him on his court-ordered visits. I feared for the mental well-being of my kids.

Once both his tactics with the State of New Hampshire's DCYF (Division of Youth and Families) and Social Services backfired, Tim did the only thing he could get away with: he moved and refused tell me where he lived or give me a phone number in case of an emergency. I had no contact with my children when they were with him, and there was nothing I could do about it. He told my children lies about what a horrible person I was and that I didn't love them or want them. In his twisted mind, he figured the more the kids hated me, the more they would love him. Not once did he ever consider the affect his behavior was having on them.

Most of what I earned went to daycare expenses and I fell $3,000 behind in my rent. I owed everyone money and even stopped answering my phone because I knew it would be a bill collector. Every day I came home wondering if my electricity or phone would be shut off. I never had the money to fill the oil tank, but my landlord always made sure the tank was full. Even though he could have evicted me, he never did. I'm sure he thought I would end up leaving in the middle of the night and never paying him, but that never happened. As soon as I received a small monetary settlement for the car accident I'd been in with Sha as a teenager, the first check I wrote was for $3,600 in back rent and oil.

For the next ten years this was my life. I struggled financially to provide for my kids, defended myself against Tim's constant allegations in court, all the while my focus was always on my children and buffering the blows of their father. I always had to be on guard; I never knew what Tim would do next. As tempted as I was to point out to the kids what an awful person he was, I never did. I was better than to stoop to his level and I hoped that as they got older they would see this for themselves.

Those who knew me knew how hard I was working to stay afloat. As difficult as these years were for me and as hateful as Tim continued to be, it was during this time that I realized the strength of the human spirit and the goodness in people. It seemed like just when I was ready to give up and I thought things couldn't get any darker, a small miracle would happen. At just the right time, I would get an anonymous card in the mail with an uplifting message and some money. I considered this food for my soul as well as my pantry. During the holidays, I would come home from work and find a bag of gifts for the kids on my porch. And even though I never signed up for the Secret Santa program in our town, the fire department always delivered presents on Christmas Eve. In the summer I would get a phone call from the Science Center on Squam Lake telling me that my kids were chosen for a full scholarship to their camp, yet I'd never applied.

It was these little things, the small blessings that kept me going. I realized that life would always have roadblocks and potholes, but if I chose to look at the small miracles along the way, it would all be worthwhile.

Somehow things always worked out for me, as if there were a "guardian angel" watching over me. And I believe there was.

Chapter Twenty-one

In late fall of 2006 I found myself in another seemingly hopeless predicament. I was in yet another custody battle with Tim, the cottage I was renting was being condemned and I was desperately trying to find an affordable place to live. I totaled my car when I slipped on the icy roads of an early snow and hit a guard rail. Thankfully no one was hurt (except my wallet). I didn't have automobile insurance. It was the first new car I ever owned and I still had three years left to pay on it.

It seemed like no matter how hard I worked I just couldn't get ahead. Every time the phone rang I feared it would be a bill collector about my car so I all but stopped answering the telephone. I just wanted something good to happen in my life for once.

Just when I thought things couldn't get worse, they did. On this particular day my phone wouldn't stop ringing. Who ever was calling would hang up and call again. After about the sixth time I reluctantly picked it up.

"Hello," I said in a rather annoyed tone.

"Don't you ever answer the goddamn phone," a familiar voice shouted from the other end.

"Hi Bill," I responded as I rolled my eyes. *Great, what now*, I thought.

"What's the deal, you can't even take time to talk to the man who raised your ass," he barked.

"I was just heading out the door to pick up the kids," I lied. "What's up?"

"I need you to get your shit out of my storage unit."

"Bill, I'm right in the middle of having to move, I'm using a borrowed car, I really don't have any place to put it," I pleaded. "Does it have to be done now?"

"I called your brothers too. Anything you kids don't come and take is going to the dump, I don't need the f****** bill every month. Its not like you guys have been chipping in," he yelled, clearly not caring that I was in a bad situation at the moment.

"Fine, I'll try to get over there this weekend."

After a few minutes of listening to Bill whine about how I never come to see him I hung up frustrated that I now had one more thing I needed to worry about doing. Sometimes it just all becomes to overwhelming and my little "vice" is the only relief I have.

The next weekend I had off from my nursing job I went over to the storage unit and grabbed the few boxes I had. Most of the stuff was from my teenage years when Bill had to move off the farm after the feds seized it. I couldn't even remember what was in the boxes. Actually, I couldn't wait to get home and open them and see.

The first box had mostly old clothes. The next one I opened was filled with mementoes and trinkets from my youth, like the Monchichi doll Bill had gotten me when I was ten-years old. That was the last Christmas I'd had with my mom. For a few minutes I was taken back to my childhood. When I flipped open the last box I saw that it was mostly paperwork and files. Figuring I must have inadvertently grabbed something of Bills I started to close it up but something shinny caught my eye. It was a necklace with a solid gold pendant with the scales of justice embedded in it. I knew immediately whose it was. My mother's and she had been wearing it the night she'd died. Over the years in all my moves I had lost the locket with a strand of my mother's hair that was given to me at her funeral. As I held it tightly in my hand I stared at it, imagining the horror the last time she wore it.

As I pawed through the rest of the things in the box I realized the paperwork was copies of various notes and motions submitted by both the prosecution and defense from my mom's murder trial. Most of it I had already read when I'd gone to the Grafton County Court house years before. But as fate would have it there was one vital document I had not yet seen. I opened the legal-sized envelope and realized it was Suds' psychological evaluation.

Relieved that my kids weren't home from school I poured myself a glass of red wine and sat down to read the report.

Steven 'Suds' Sudvari was the youngest of three children whose mother died of a brain tumor when Suds was only six years old. He had a special bond with his older sister who became a mother figure to him. Up until he was fourteen years old, it seemed that he had a relatively unremarkable childhood, other then experiencing the loss of his mom. He had lots of friends, played sports and had a close relationship with his dad and siblings. His performance in school was lackluster, however, and he repeated the second and seventh grades.

When his father remarried eight years after his mother's death, Suds got along well with his step-mom Anna and three step siblings. He recalls that he was very happy during that time, which lasted only a year. When his step-mom abandoned the family he became enraged. Anna not only left the family, taking her own children with her, but she took all the family's money, leaving Suds' father deep in debt. His feelings of rejection and anger persisted for a few months, during which time Suds told his father he was willing to burn her house down and kill her.

Having become depressed with his life, he reports that he began drinking and became an alcoholic at the age of fifteen. Despite his popularity and social activities, he dated very little during his adolescence and had no close relationships with any female other than his sister. During his senior year of high school, Suds dropped out and enlisted in the Air Force. From

January of 1971 to January of 1972, he was assigned to a radar station at Quang Tri, six miles below the demilitarized zone in Vietnam. He was a noncombatant, did not carry weapons and saw no actual combat, and lost no close friends. It turned out to be a relatively safe and uneventful assignment. He states that the vulnerability of his station made him feel "terrified of death all the time." He used drugs heavily during that period, especially alcohol, heroin, stimulants and cannabis. He believes his Vietnam experience is responsible for "a lot of bad attitudes" such as his subsequent drug problems, his family problems, his inability to accept authority and therefore hold a steady job, and his inability to trust anyone.

His discharge from the military was a result of his refusal to accept the discipline of a stateside assignment. Following his discharge, he reports his life as a "blur," centered mostly on acquiring, selling and taking psychoactive drugs. Although he states that he has not taken heroin since leaving the service, he has been a very heavy user of alcohol, stimulants, cannabis, LSD and PCP. He reports that his continuous use of such substances helps him to feel less depressed and forget his problems.

Although he does have alcoholic blackouts, he states that he rarely becomes violent and reports that he did stop drinking for a time and didn't resume until after the homicide. He states that stimulants (cocaine, caffeine, speed) keep him going, give him an energy kick but also, at times, make him paranoid. He reports that while he has used significant amounts of these drugs over the years, it increased considerably after his girlfriend Cathy left him two months before the homicide.

LSD was used heavily between 1972 and 1977. He states, "I tripped four to five times a week and took close to three hundred acid trips in all." He denies ever having a bad trip, hallucinations or persecutory delusions. Instead, he reports that LSD "seemed to heighten the thrill of everything and produced pleasant visual illusions."

"PCP never produced the pleasant feelings I had on acid," he states, adding that with PCP there were lots of visual hallucinations and perceptual distortions. "PCP took me away from reality so I didn't have to pay attention to my problems." He states that he usually had amnesia with most PCP experiences. He reportedly did PCP several times a week during the past few years and his use increased significantly following Cathy's departure. He recalls taking PCP on the morning of the homicide but reports amnesia for most of what followed. The only thing about the actual homicide that he recalls is stabbing Patty four times in the back and feeling emotionally detached from that action. He remembers her asking him, "Why?" and his inability to answer. He denies any recollection of his subsequent brutal assault on Patty Keefe. He reports a fearful awareness of what he had done some time after the murder and reports that his dominant emotion was fear and his cognitive focus was escape.

Sudvari denies that he had any strong feelings toward Patty. "She was an attractive woman who was part of the group centered around Bill's home and business." The woman he found most attractive, other than Cathy, was Linda. "I don't think I would have killed Patty if Cathy hadn't left. I had nothing against Patty. More likely, I would have killed Cathy."

Psychologically, the most important event in his life was his relationship with Cathy. She was the first and only woman in his life with whom he was able to sustain a prolonged and intimate relationship. Abandonment and rejection from women had been a major fear throughout his life due to his mother's death and step-mother's desertion and ultimately the break-up of his own relationship with Cathy when she returned to her former life.

It has been noted by all of Sudvari's friends that he underwent a significant transformation during the years he was with Cathy. He began to feel better about himself, started caring about his appearance and began making plans and commitments about the future. The one major source of tension in the relationship was with Cathy's child, who lived with her ex-husband in Pennsylvania. The ex-husband was always regarded as serious competition and Sudvari feared that Cathy would ultimately go back to him and her old life. When she did return to Pennsylvania it exacerbated the age-old conviction that women were "hateful" and a "bunch of sluts who invite love and then abandon you forever." Such intense ambivalence manifested itself during the course of their relationship.

Around Christmas 1980, his self-fulfilling prophecy came true when Cathy left. She returned briefly in January 1981 but then left again. "After that I was never straight," he reports. "She was a part of me and I missed her." His state of mind oscillated between rage and depression. He frequently thought of suicide and it is possible that such a heightened ingestion of stimulants was his attempt at self-medicating. His rage toward Cathy was exhibited by his brutal killing of her cat two weeks before the homicide. His intense ambivalence towards her is exemplified by the fact that he wept and petted the dead cat afterwards.

The conclusion of the report states that "PCP most likely produced an intensification of angry feelings and would have induced aggressive behavior. Suds' reports of perceptual distortions, motor in-coordination, amnesia, emotional detachment and violent behavior are consistent with PCP intoxication. Believing that Suds' ingestion of PCP was a necessary but not sufficient condition for murder, we are forced to speculate on what happened by putting the pieces of the puzzle together based on the accounts of different people. His emotional response to the rejection he felt when Cathy left was also a necessary but insufficient reason for his violent response. Killing Cathy's cat was the closest Suds had ever come to being violent. There was no evidence of post-traumatic stress disorder, chronic or delayed, resulting from Suds' experience in Vietnam."

Given all the information at hand, the psychologist hypothesized that on the morning of my mother's murder, February 26, 1981, after everyone else had gone, Sudvari made a sexual advance which she rejected. This resulted in the last straw for a man who had hated and distrusted women all his life. At that moment my mom became representative of all women and Suds unleashed his rage, brought on in part by PCP. It became uncontrollable and although he most likely knew he was killing my mom, he really wanted to kill Cathy.

After reading the six-page report, I felt like the wind had been knocked out of me. This man had tried to blame the vicious murder of my mom on his childhood (which was relatively normal, except for the natural death of his mother), being in the military and breaking up with his girlfriend. The defense had tried to use post-traumatic stress disorder from Suds' time in Vietnam as his reason for killing my mother and, in fact, the reason for all his problems, including drugs. This made no sense to me. Suds had never been violent before when under the influence of PCP, so what had made him snap that time? My childhood had sucked far worse than his, but I'd never resorted to murder or any other form of criminal activity. What a copout! But isn't that what people do? Blame their childhood for their problems and failures as adults. That was something I swore never to do, use my childhood as an excuse.

Each time I endeavored to find answers and closure, I found myself with more questions and yet another door to open. I still needed to hear the words from the man responsible and to know, after all these years, if he remembered anything else. I wondered if he was remorseful. It had been seventeen years since I'd last made contact with him and it was about time I did so again. He would now be in his fifties.

Chapter Twenty-two

Suds' response to my inquiry to meet with him was very simple: "The prison now has a victim service coordinator and you need to contact him for a meeting."

For five months, I met with mediators, facilitators and psychologists. Before my meeting with Suds could take place, I had to prove that I was a competent and emotionally stable adult. I had to provide names of people close to me who could serve as character witnesses and vouch for my healthy state of mind. I chose my mother's best friend Nard and my best friend Sha.

Finally the day came when I would come face-to-face with the man who had changed my life's course. After years of doing research, discovering truths (some of which I could live with and others I still didn't understand) and thinking about this man, a cold criminal, it finally came down to this, the moment of truth. How would I react when I saw him again after all those years? Would I even recognize him?

On a beautiful, sunny February morning I traveled down Interstate 93. *She's no longer with us* were the words echoing in my head as our car entered the parking area. The sign read "New Hampshire State Correctional Facility." Observing the barbwire and electric fence around the perimeter, the realization of what I was about to do suddenly became overwhelming. Trembling with uncertainty, knowing I had waited so long for this day, for a moment I wondered if I could accomplish what I'd set out to do. My heart was racing and my chest felt like it was in a vice. Breathing became an effort and everything seemed surreal as I sat staring at the massive brick compound.

When I finally got out of the car, my legs felt like jelly. My hands were shaking, my stomach was gurgling and I felt dizzy. I'd never been more nervous in my life. As I regained my composure, I reminded myself why I was there. The questions that had been haunting me for most of my life were about to be answered. I was only minutes away from meeting the man responsible for my mother's death.

I was thankful my best friend Sha was with me offering her unconditional support (and a Xanax). She had been by my side every step of the journey that had brought me here. As we slowly approached the entrance to the prison, the anticipation was almost unbearable.

"I am here for a facilitation with inmate Steven Sudvari," I told the short, dark-haired woman behind the Plexiglass window.

She passed a clipboard through a small opening and said, "Print your name, date and time of arrival and sign at the bottom."

It was at that moment that I realized the irony of this day, February 26, 2007. Exactly twenty-six years ago to the day, Suds had brutally murdered my mom.

Startled by the clanking of the thick metal door unlocking, Sha and I jumped. The guard chuckled at our uneasiness as he motioned us through. A combination of excitement and apprehension filled me. We made our way deeper into the prison. Every sound, every smell was cold and unforgiving. Prisoners in their traditional orange jumpsuits roamed about the courtyard. As we were led to the Chapel area where the meeting would take place, we spotted guards atop the buildings, clutching rifles as they surveyed every inch of the grounds.

My mind wandered back to a time when I was eleven years old, the last time I'd set eyes on this man. A man who had worked for my step-dad on the farm and even babysat us kids a few times. That final image was of a tall, lanky, twenty-nine-year-old man entering the courtroom, his hands and feet shackled. When our eyes had met across the room, the hair on the back of my neck had stood on end. He'd made my skin crawl. I remembered him, with a smirk on his face, making the gesture of slicing his throat, and my being forced to leave and wait outside for the remainder of my mom's trial. Seeing him that day in the courtroom made me feel as though I was looking at pure evil.

Now, as we sat waiting at the round table in the chapel conference room, I felt numb. It was surreal. I didn't know how I would feel when I saw him. I understood that, although I could ask the burning questions, there was a good chance he'd lie to me. I clutched my notebook containing everything I wanted to know. I was doing something no one else in my family had the courage to do.

There were five chairs. The prison chaplain sat to my right, Sha sat to my left and the facilitator sat next to her. There was a pitcher of water, paper cups and a box of tissues in the center of the table. Across from me was an empty chair waiting to be filled by the man I'd waited twenty-five years to confront.

Soon I heard the shuffling of feet echoing down the corridor. I wondered what I would do, how I would react in the presence of a killer. It seemed to take forever, but suddenly he was standing in the doorway. Gasping for breath, he looked as if he might collapse as he held onto the wall for support. A wave of relief swept over me. I didn't find him scary, and I didn't see him as a killer. On that day he appeared to be a sick old man with shoulder-length grey hair and a matching mustache that hung into his mouth. He sported a large pot belly and could barely walk. I grabbed Sha's knee. She placed her hand on mine reassuringly.

Feeling as though I were watching the event from afar, I stood up from my chair and extended my hand. "Thank you for meeting with me."

For the next two hours I looked him straight in the eye as he answered my questions. I never even realized that I was nervously picking at my left thumb nail, a habit I'd started after my mom died which over the years has caused a permanent indentation in that nail. My first question was the same one my mother had asked him before taking her last breath: "Why?"

His answer was still the same. "I don't know."

"She was the one person who was good to you," I reminded him. "Did you ever think you would kill her?"

Visibly shaken and twisting his fingers together nervously, he responded, "No."

He became emotional when I asked, "If you were truly psychotic, why didn't you kill my little brother, too?"

Tears welled up in his eyes. "I thought I did."

Hearing him say that traumatized me. All that time he was on the run, he believed he had killed a two-year-old baby. It was at that point that my hatred for him turned to pity and my compassion came to the forefront.

"I always knew I would face off with someone from your family," Suds admitted.

Had my attitude been different that day, I believe I would have gotten some different responses from him. The fact that I wasn't mean, hateful or nasty seemed to affect him, and that was why he displayed so much emotion. There were times during our meeting when Suds had to stop and compose himself to avoid breaking down. I wasn't prepared for such a sincere display of emotion. I believe he was truly remorseful.

One of the things I learned that day, which horrified me the most, was that within hours of his arrest for my mother's brutal murder, the Feds showed up and offered him a deal.

"They told me that if I gave them everything I knew about Bill, they would cut me a deal and give me a manslaughter charge instead of first degree murder," he explained to me in a nervous voice.

This meant he would have served a maximum of fifteen years while my brothers and I served a life sentence. I was stunned that the cops would bargain like that, given the brutality of the crime. Suds hadn't shot or stabbed my mother only once; he'd viciously attacked her for two hours. And they had been willing to label it manslaughter so they could get the goods on somebody they thought was a major drug dealer. At that point, I was angrier at the Feds and their blatant disregard for human life than I was at this man sitting across from me, who had so brutally taken my mother's life.

After I showed him pictures of my brothers and told him we were all happy and productive adults, Suds said, "I'm really glad you kids didn't grow up consumed with anger at what I did. I always hoped that you'd be able to move past it."

"You took away the only unconditional love my brothers and I knew. And you, of all people, should understand that because your mother died when you were little."

Clearing his throat and gathering his composure, it took him a few attempts to respond. "I know. I'm sorry," he said. "I deserve to be in prison until I die, and I believe my true punishment won't come until after that."

"Oh, what'd he find, God?" I said sarcastically to the prison Chaplin.

"No," he replied.

At that point I was at odds with myself. Part of me wanted to get angry and another part wanted to reach out to him and say, "It's okay." I'd never felt compassion quite like that before, and it scared me. I even felt guilty about feeling so badly for him.

As we were leaving, I said to Sha, "What's the matter with me? This man viciously murdered my mother and I feel bad for him."

"It's called forgiveness, Jen," she said. "This is all part of the healing process, and you have nothing to feel guilty about. It took a lot of strength and courage for you to come here today, and you should be proud of yourself. Now you can lock that door to your past and move forward."

It took me days to fully process the meeting and to realize that my ability to feel sorry for him had come from my making so many mistakes in my own life. I knew that one bad choice could change your whole life. Even though I had never murdered anyone, I knew what it was like. While I think he had premeditated ripping off the farm, I don't think he ever thought about killing my mother. I believe his action was a byproduct of his madness from the drugs.

Suds never told me why he chose to take my mom's life, but I do think there was something he intended to tell me that day. Even the facilitators knew there was something else because at the meeting's close each of them asked, "Isn't there something you want to tell Jennifer?" Both times his response was, "No." Despite this, meeting with him brought me peace and closure. This process ignited a desire in me to become a victim's advocate and help others who were going through a similar situation.

Only weeks after my meeting with Suds, I received a call from the prison Chaplin who informed me that Suds was lying in his bed waiting to die. His heart was getting weaker and he was refusing medical treatment. I couldn't help but wonder if my visit had meant closure for him, too, and had brought him the peace he needed to finally leave this earth. I recalled his comment that his true sentence wouldn't come until he died. I don't know if that is true or not, but if twenty-five years in prison isn't punishment enough, the eternity of hell must be unimaginable.

As I sat contemplating his imminent demise, I wondered if he was conscious or in a coma. What thoughts and images were preoccupying him as he lay trapped in the final days between life and death?

Chapter Twenty-three

As I walked to the car after my daughter's lacrosse game, I glanced at my cell phone and noticed I'd missed a call and had a message. Wondering why I hadn't heard the phone ring, I dialed my voicemail, figuring it must be my boyfriend Steve.

It had been over twelve years since my divorce and my relationship with Steve was the first one I'd had that didn't make me feel like I was suffocating. For years and years after my divorce, being in a relationship was an anxiety-ridden experience for me. I only dated guys I knew would be around for a short while. We'd have some fun and that would be it, which was fine with me. I wasn't looking for anything long term. I'd made a promise to myself years earlier that my kids where the only relationship I needed. On the rare occasion that I did date nice, respectable guys, I would soon find fault and have to break up with them. Eventually, my friends caught on to my pattern and said, "What's wrong with this one, Jen? Back too hairy? Pooped in your bathroom? Blew his nose in front of you?"

I guess I had pretty vain reasons for breaking up with someone, but subconsciously I was afraid to make the same mistake I'd made with my ex-husband, or the same mistake my mother had made by staying with Bill. It was safer this way. But with Steve it was different. We'd been friends for years and then one day something clicked. (We have been dating for over a year now, which is quite a feat for me). I have yet to find a petty complaint about Steve or feel like I want to run and hide before I fall completely and madly in love with him and risk getting hurt when he betrays me like everyone else in my life—Tim, my brother, friends and family. This time, I refuse to let fear or past experiences ruin my relationship with Steve. For the first time in my life, I feel complete and can actually envision my future, the rest of my life, with this one person.

As I continued to walk past the hockey rink and cafeteria of the New Hampton Prep School that my fifteen-year-old daughter attended, an unfamiliar voice came over the phone. It had been three months since I'd been to the prison to meet with Suds. And although I was still a bit haunted by the whole experience I was slowly starting to feel a sense of relief and closure to my past. I continued walking toward my car while listening to the voicemail on my cell phone. As soon as I realized that it wasn't Steve I stopped in my tracks.

"This is Dr. Kaplan calling from Melrose-Wakefield Hospital. Your father is back in ICU and I need you to contact me right away."

Quickly I call back. Being a nurse, I knew from experience that when a doctor personally called a family member, it wasn't good news.

"Melrose-Wakefield Hospital," said the friendly voice on the other end.

"I'm calling to speak with Dr. Kaplan," I said nervously.

"Oh, yes. Hold on, please," she said before putting me on hold.

"Dr. Kaplan," a soft masculine voice intoned.

"This is Jen, Jimmy Keefe's daughter."

"Thank you for calling back," he replied. "Your father arrived in the emergency room with severe vomiting and abdominal pain early this morning. We need to make some decisions. When can you get down here?"

"I'm not sure I can get to Massachusetts until tomorrow morning," I said, wavering inside between being annoyed and feeling guilty.

"Unfortunately I don't think he will be alive by morning," the doctor said emphatically.

I could tell the color had drained from my face by the look on my daughter's face. She had been watching me intently, trying to figure out who I was talking to and what was going on. When I got off the phone with Dr.

Kaplan, I immediately called my brother James and explained what was happening. My dad was going to die and it scared me. He was my last living parent and although he hadn't been much of one, just knowing he was out there was a comfort.

After working out all the details about where my kids would be so I could go to Massachusetts and see my dad for the last time, I figured I would stay overnight at my Nana's. Unexpectedly, my brother called back and said he wanted to come with me, despite the fact that it was eight o'clock at night. I was happy to have some alone time with James. It had been years since we really spent any quality time together and, an hour later we were on the road — after stopping to buy a six-pack for the ride (in honor of my dad, of course). Heading south on Interstate 93, we arrived at the hospital at 9:30 PM.

When the elevator doors opened, I saw many strange yet familiar faces sitting in chairs outside the ICU: my dad's brother and his wife, whom I hadn't seen in fourteen years; my dad's present girlfriend, who was falling apart; and his ex-girlfriend, with whom he had remained close friends.

"Hello," a young doctor I dubbed Doogie Howser MD said, as he extended his hand. "You must be the eldest daughter I spoke with on the phone."

"Yes, I'm Jennifer, and this is my brother James," I responded nervously.

"Your father's liver disease has progressed. He still has the GI bleed and his cancer has spread—"

Wait a minute! Liver failure? Cancer? I didn't know about any of this.

"Last time he was here I was told his liver function test came back fine," I interrupted.

"Yes, well, it seems his liver was worse than we originally thought."

"I didn't know anything about cancer, either," I said.

"I'm very sorry I don't have better news for you. I will leave you with your family to talk about your plan of action." With that, he exited the waiting room.

"I'm going in to see my dad," I said.

I sat in the ICU looking at my biological father Jimmy while a respirator breathed for him. He was hooked up to machines with wires that monitored his vital signs—heart rate, oxygen level and blood pressure. Having been a geriatric nurse for ten years, I knew that the numbers displayed on the monitors weren't good. Dried blood was caked around his nose and mouth, evidence of the days of vomiting the doctor had informed me about. Apparently, six months ago he had been diagnosed with advanced-stage bone cancer but had refused treatment. A month ago he'd been back with an acute GI bleed and was admitted into the hospital for a few days. Upon his release, the doctor told him that if he didn't stop drinking the bleed would get worse and possibly rupture, which it did.

My head was clouded by so many different thoughts. I was angry that my dad hadn't told anyone about his cancer, not even his girlfriend. I was furious that he'd given up again. I felt guilty that I hadn't come down a couple of months earlier when he was in the hospital, and was sad that this would be the last time I'd ever see him.

James and I sat on opposite sides of the hospital bed, each holding one of his hands. His skin was yellowish and he was cold and clammy. Being a nurse, I knew what that meant; the end was very near. As the sound of the heart monitor beeped, I wondered what, if anything, was going through his mind. Did he know that James and I were there? I glanced at my brother. He had the look I recall seeing only once before, when our dad told us that our mom was gone.

"What are you thinking?" I ask him, interrupting his thoughts.

"That I should have made more of an effort to see Dad over the years."

"I knew he was going to drink himself to death. I just never imagined I'd feel this way," I replied.

"Yeah. I don't even remember the last time I told him I loved him," James said with a pained look on his face. "I feel like I have so much I want to say now that it's too late."

"Me, too," I said before turning my thoughts back to my dad and reflecting on my childhood, the one he'd hardly been a part of. I thought about all the things I'd say to him if I had the chance.

Despite the fact that my father hadn't directly influenced my life, he was still the person responsible for giving me life, which meant more to me than I'd realized. I was overwhelmed with a tidal wave of emotions as I stared at his frail body. He had turned fifty-eight the month before, but years of a liquid diet made him look twice that. As I sat holding his hand, I tried to remember the last time I had seen him. Living much like a transient, my dad had spent his life sitting on a bar stool at the American Legion living off unemployment and crashing on the couches of various friends. Whenever I happened to be in town visiting my Nana, I'd stop by the Legion to see him. If he wasn't there, the cashier at the local package store would tell me where to locate him.

After leaving the hospital, James and I sat in the parking lot trying to process all that had transpired over the past few hours. The sight of my dad lying there—no smile, no jokes; just his chest going up and down artificially, courtesy of a machine—was hard to take. A knot formed in my throat when I recalled my brother, child-like, tenderly stroking my dad's head and whispering, "You've really got yourself all f***** up now, Dad." I turned and looked out the passenger-side window so James wouldn't see the tears welling up.

Driving back to New Hampshire was a quiet ride. Without saying a word, we both knew this was it. Now we would just wait for the call. It was after two-thirty in the morning when I arrived home. Exhausted, I went straight to bed. When I awoke a few hours later, I immediately called the hospital.

"This is Jennifer Keefe calling about my father, Jimmy Keefe."

"Oh, yes, we were just getting ready to call you. I'm sorry but your father coded and passed away ten minutes ago," the nurse said matter-of-factly.

"Um, thank you," I said before hanging up the phone.

I was stunned. Even though I knew his death was inevitable, the shock of hearing the words took my breath away. After letting the realization that I was now an orphan sink in, I immediately thought about the arrangements and wondered who would be responsible. Being the oldest child, I knew I should step up to the plate and take care of it myself. It would have been the right thing to do. But I didn't. How could I? What kind of example had my dad set about "stepping up to the plate?"

For someone who doesn't allow feelings to surface, I felt like I was on an emotional rollercoaster. I was angry with myself for not taking more initiative to see my dad over the years and angry with him for not doing the same. Then the anger turned to regret that I would never have the opportunity to make peace with my dad or to understand why he'd turned his back on James and me. And then guilt washed over me for having dismissed him over the years because I'd felt abandoned and rejected. Then came the sadness. I felt a tug at my heart. My dad had died alone, no doubt with a barrel of regrets.

Refusing to let these emotions get the better of me, I quickly diverted my thoughts. If I kept myself busy I wouldn't have to think about how I was feeling. After making several phone calls to my brother, my Nana and Auntie, as well as to my dad's girlfriend, I waited to hear from my dad's brother regarding the details of the service. Two days went by before anyone called me and I started to get very angry. Isn't that how it had always been? Out of sight, out of mind. Finally, on the day of the "calling hours," when friends, family and acquaintances could pay their respects, I was informed of the arrangements that had been made. The calling hours would be from 6:00 PM to 9:00 PM at the funeral home in Wakefield.

After scrambling to make arrangements for my kids (who didn't want to attend) and throwing some clothes in a bag, I started out on my two-hour drive back to Massachusetts. If all went well, I would arrive at about 6:00 PM. Being the oldest daughter, I felt I should be there with the rest of the family, James said he'd meet me there. When I arrived, I saw people I knew but hadn't seen in twenty-six years, since my mother's funeral. It was comforting to be around folks who had known both my parents, especially when they kept saying things like "You look just like your mother." That was something I'd never grown up hearing, and it was nice for a change. At the same time, it was bittersweet. I enjoyed hearing people compare me to her, but it made me miss her more. And when they said things like "Your father was so proud of you. He loved you very much and talked about you all the time," I couldn't stop the tidal wave of emotion from surfacing again. I was glad to hear that my dad actually thought about me over the years, but why hadn't he told me those things himself? Another bittersweet moment.

I was shocked when my dad's girlfriend came up to me and said with utmost sincerity, "You know, Jen, your dad is exactly where he has always wanted to be—in heaven with your mother." Her comment was like a punch in the stomach and literally took my breath away. Had my dad loved my mom that much? Had he lived all these years merely existing, waiting to die so he could see her again?

For the rest of the night, I numbly went through the motions, waiting for it to be over. I needed to be alone so I could process everything I was feeling. Every time someone commented on how much my dad had loved me or how he was finally in heaven with my mom, a piece of the protective wall I'd put up when I was a child would start to crumble. I could feel the tears begin to well up, but I refused to let them flow.

My father looked better in his casket than he did that last time I saw him barely alive in the hospital. He looked so peaceful with his Red Sox jersey and baseball cap. As I stood looking down at him, I noticed that a season's ticket dated April 20th (his birthday) had been placed in his hands. Along the rim of the maple casket were four number seven playing cards, one from each suit. A combination laugh / cry escaped my lips when I realized they were from his poker buddies.

"If there was a six-pack of Budweiser in there with him, Dad would be at his happiest," James said coming up behind me.

I knew he was trying to be funny to lighten the mood, but all I could do was look at him through the tears in my eyes that I refused to let flow. Swallowing hard to erase the lump in my throat, I turned to mingle with the rest of the friends and family who had come to pay their respects. There must have been close to a hundred people, most of them friends of my dad's since grade school, which meant they'd known my mom, too, and had been at her funeral as well. It was very reminiscent of the last time I'd been in the very same funeral home at the age of ten, when the person lying in the coffin had been my mom. I was freaked out by the flashbacks I was having and couldn't wait for the night to be over.

On my way to my Nana's house after the calling hours, I stopped by the corner market and picked up a six-pack in memory of my dad. I was all alone and needed to do one last thing before calling it a night. I headed over to the cemetery to see my mom. For some reason, I felt the need to share my dad's death with her. I hadn't been there in years and wasn't sure I could find the gravesite. After much searching, I finally found her plot and sat down next to her headstone. As I lit a cigarette and popped open a beer, I said, "I have to say, Mom, I'm a little jealous that Dad is up there with you now. The thought of the two of you sitting in heaven catching up makes me envious." The image of my parents sitting high above on a cloud looking down at me was surreal.

I stayed for about half an hour, thinking about my life, my parents' life and everything that had happened since my mother's death. I had so many questions about them that would never be answered now. I had always been very good at hiding my feelings, but this time I had no control over the things that were surfacing and it scared me. This time I couldn't just put on my happy face and pretend it didn't bother me. I was sad that my dad was gone and angry that I'd heard things from virtual strangers that he himself should have told me. I regretted the fact that I would never have the opportunity to tell him what I thought or ask him my burning questions.

The next day was cold and dreary, very fitting for a funeral and yet another reminder of my mother's death. The services were held at the same Catholic Church. I suspected there would be as many people at my dad's funeral as there had been at my mom's. Twenty-five years ago, this church had been packed so full that people had to stand against the wall and in the foyer. But today, for my dad, there were only about twenty close friends and family.

When the priest began the service I couldn't help but wonder if this was really what my father would have wanted. He was never a very religious man. I'm sure he would much rather have had his funeral at the American Legion, where everyone could celebrate his life with a beer rather than mourn it in a church he probably hadn't been in since my mother's funeral. As I listened to the sermon about life and how we are all here for a purpose, I wondered what my dad's purpose had been. It wasn't like he had done anything really extraordinary. In fact, he had done nothing but cause me to feel pain and rejection my whole life. When the priest intoned that our time on earth is spent touching the lives of others, people we don't even realize we impact, I wondered whose lives my dad had impacted. The clerks at the liquor store? What legacy had he left behind? My dad was an alcoholic, a weak man who'd given up his children. What the priest was saying didn't seem to fit my dad. How could it? He hadn't known my dad. Even so, it was all very thought-provoking and forced me to analyze my own life. What was *my* purpose?

Chapter Twenty-four

The emotions and feelings that were stirring inside me, wanting desperately to be free, finally became stronger than my ability to keep them suppressed. Once they came out, they wouldn't stop, and for the next few days all I did was cry. I was back in New Hampshire by then but kept replaying the events of the past few days. Each time it hurt a little more and I began to wonder if I was losing my mind. Why was the death of my dad, a man I'd hardly seen and who'd had no direct influence on my life, causing me so much pain? Why couldn't I stop crying? I wasn't just thinking about my dad; I was thinking about my mom, too.

"I think what's happening to you is that you are mourning both your parents' deaths," my friend Sha said over the phone. "When you were little, you weren't given the opportunity to grieve such a significant loss and you have held it in all these years."

"It's just all so sad," I said as I started to cry again. "I feel so weak."

"Well, I don't think you should look at this as weakness, Jen. It would be easier for you to act like none of this mattered, like your dad didn't matter. Weakness is taking the easy way out of dealing with the pain and doing what you've always done, bottling it up. It takes a lot of strength to still love your dad in spite of the disappointment he has brought you."

"I don't feel strong. And you know me...I don't cry, either," I said, angry at myself for becoming so emotional. "I'm a real orphan now, Sha. I have so much I want to say to my dad, now that I can't."

"Well, write him a letter then. Sometimes it helps to put your feelings on paper. It allows you an outlet to get it out of your head so you can move forward. If you think about it, everything has come full circle for you. You've spent the last few years getting to know who your mom was, finding the answers to her death, and now you've been given the opportunity to understand a side of your dad you didn't know. If you can find even one positive thing about each circumstance in your life and in your parents' lives, then you've accomplished something and you should be thankful for that."

"You know how much I hate getting in touch with my feelings," I said with a half-hearted laugh. "And the crying...well, that's just pissing me off."

"Believe me, I know, Jen. The only other time I've seen you cry is when we were roommates as teenagers and our telephone was shut off because we couldn't afford to pay the bill. But seriously, I admire you for having the strength to face all of this head-on. I mean it when I say that you should be proud of yourself. You're the most courageous person I know."

"After all this, you know what my advice to people who have a strained relationship with a parent would be. To fix it before it's too late. Once death makes that choice for you, all you're left with is regret. And that's far worse than whatever issues separate you."

"That's great advice, Jen. If you have regret for the past and no hope for the future, then you have nothing. Your life has been a testament to those around you. I for one have drawn strength from your life. Don't stop now. Take your own advice so you can finally close the door to your past and move toward your future. There are still other people in your life who have hurt and betrayed you. Fix it now, before it's too late."

When I got off the phone I decided to take Sha's advice and write my dad a letter.

Dear Dad,

There are so many subjects you and I have never discussed. Mainly how, in good conscience, you could let another man raise your children. For all the disappointment my mother felt throughout your relationship, none was as bad as the disappointment she would have felt watching you turn your back on your own children. It was one thing when she was alive, but I was only ten years old when she died.

I remember when your divorce was final and Mom tried to explain to me that the two of you knew each other too well. That was something that confused me for many years. Now I realize what she meant. She knew you lacked the strength to change your addictive ways and put your family first. All these years I viewed you as selfish and weak. The consequences of your choice must have been a fate worse than death. Alcohol consumed you and destroyed your marriage, your family and ultimately your health.

After attending your funeral and listening to your friends talk about you and seeing my step-sisters and how they turned out just like you, with addictions and consumed by their failures, I realized that it took a lot of strength to do what you did. As twisted as it seems, in spite of the lifestyle Bill led, you sacrificed your relationship with James and me in order to make sure we had a life better than what you could provide. You did what you did out of love. Since your death I have wondered what legacy you've left. I now know that my ability to persevere comes from watching you. From your weakness I took strength, and from that I found comfort.

After that, I kept writing, allowing myself to release the things I wanted to say to everyone else in my family but couldn't say in person. I never realized how much those things had been holding me back until I allowed myself to let them go.

I wrote the next letter to my Auntie and my Nana. I've always lumped them together because they've always lived together and made all their decisions pertaining to my brothers and me together. Ever since my mother died, I have been hurt and angry with them for not taking custody of us. As an adult, I've always felt they judged me for being a divorced, single parent. But now I see everything in my life from a whole new perspective. I have a freer, clearer view and realize that I can't blame them any longer for the choice they made.

Dear Auntie and Nana,

My relationship with you has been forced and superficial, to say the least. I have lived my whole life feeling like you look at me as an obligation rather than a niece or granddaughter. Growing up I couldn't understand why you never stepped forward to take my brothers and me away from the farm. I have to be honest. I felt rejected and abandoned by you, more then I did by my dad, and have carried that for most of my life.

I always felt like our "family" and those damned to help us failed the task of raising and shaping who we've become, that the people who can take credit for instilling in us the morals and values we have are of no blood relation. They came into our life, planted a seed and were gone in the blink of an eye. I've never understood why I wasn't worthy of your investment. When I became a single parent raising two young children on my own while putting myself through nursing school, I thought I had proven myself to you.

But now that I am older and looking at my childhood with a new perspective, I realize that perhaps it was the guilt the both of you carried about where you sent me after my mother's death that has created the strained relationship we have today. I suppose all the resentment I've harbored toward you all these years is unwarranted. You are not my mother, and despite her willing my brothers and me to you in the event of her death, you couldn't see past your own grief to even know we needed comfort. The tragedy of her demise must have been so devastating for you that you could not see us through your own pain.

More importantly, if you had fought to keep custody of us, you most likely would have only gotten James and me since Bill is Jason's biological father. Therefore, you would have separated us, and my mother's only wish was that all three of her children stay together. So now I realize that as hard as it must have been for you to send us back to New Hampshire, it would have been even harder to go against my mother's wish. So thank you for honoring my mom and allowing us to stay together.

Since the night my brother James confessed to knowing about my ex-husband's affairs, we became very distant. In fact, there were times when we went months without speaking, and when we did it was forced. This went on for years, but our father's death brought us together again and has started to heal the wound.

Dear James,

I have taken to letter-writing. It's a great tool for conveying my inner thoughts, and your letter is my most important one. I know you are probably thinking I'm wacky but I'm not, and that's the point of this letter. As crazy as it sounds, I have finally found myself. Learning the truth about Mom's death and Dad's recent passing has forced me to put everything into perspective and see what's important: family.

I know that you and I have been distant for many years now, and I am half to blame for that. However, the older I get the more I need to be close to you again. When we were kids, we were as close as twins. We never fought and were each other's best friend. We were so in tune with one another that it was scary. We often had the same dream or felt the other's pain. I remember the time Bill punched you in the chest for wrestling with Jason and I literally lost my breath when I saw that. And the time we were four-wheeling. You were driving and I was holding on for dear life as you popped wheelies and jumped over trees and ditches. At one point you lost control and I went flying off the back as you tipped over and the muffler burned your arm. You were more concerned with me than with your own injuries.

It's funny, I have a perception of our childhood which is quite different from your, yet we lived through the same horrible events. I know you thought Bill spoiled me growing up and that I always got my way. But you were so laid back that you did whatever Bill said. You never argued with him. I on the other hand, always fought back and knew that if I argued enough and persuaded Bill, he would eventually give in just to shut me up.

Looking back now, I realize that you were more than my best friend; you were my protector, my conscience and my only source of unconditional love. Even after we moved from the farm when I was eighteen, we continued to live together for a couple of years as roommates. I've always thought that if we took the good qualities we each possess and put them together, collectively, we'd make a perfect person. You are the other half of me and I feel incomplete without you.

Even though there are no bridges between my little brother Jason and me, I still had something I wanted to say to him. Something I have held inside for so many years for fear that it would open a wound he's not ready to heal.

Dear Jason,

My relationship with you is the healthiest of all the family members and I am thankful for that. But I worry that the scars you bear are deeper than the one left on your face—a constant reminder of that horrific night. Life has not been easy for any of us. Our childhood was stolen, and not just by the man who killed our mother. I admire your strength and loyalty and my hope is that you have found peace with the past.

When I look at you I can still see that little boy with chocolate-brown eyes running around the farm naked, giving you your nickname Buff. It's funny how that name has stayed with you even today. You have grown into a wonderful person. I'd like to believe that it is partly due to me and what I did in helping to raise you. I am so proud of the man you have become, as I'm sure Mom, looking down on you, is, too. I love you, little brother, and I hope you find healing in the truth.

Despite everything I've been through I have come to realize that I love Bill like a father. His way may have been the "School of Hard Knocks" with tough love and even tougher life lessons, but he is the one who raised me when no one else would, and, good, bad or ugly, that says a lot.

The Turkey Farm – Behind the Smile

Dear Bill,

This letter to you is the most complicated one for me to write. Growing up, I viewed you as a, money-hungry SOB whose priorities were all messed up. You catered to people who didn't matter and didn't care about the people who did. You believed that your happiness was in something you could attain, something material. You were such a difficult person to live with, but I don't think you even saw it. I always felt that you were uninvolved and unsupportive of me and I never completely felt like I was part of your family. I didn't grow up calling anyone "Mom" or "Dad," which created a huge void in my life. I blamed you and thought I hated you. In fact, I swore that once I graduated from high school I would leave the farm and you, and never come back. But even after I left, I was always drawn back. My attachment to you is something I could not explain to myself, let alone anyone else.

Now that I look back on my years at the farm, I can see the valuable tools you taught me. Growing up every second of every day was about work. As an adult I have never been afraid to work hard, and that is something you instilled in me. I attribute that to my ability to work three jobs while going to nursing school as a single parent. Instead of looking back on my childhood with regret and what-ifs, I am choosing to look at the lessons I learned from each difficult and horrific encounter.

My biggest and most shocking realization as I've gotten older is that you are the only parental connection I have. Even now, there may always be a string attached, but when I've been forced to turn to you for help you've always come through.

My final letter was the easiest to write because I finally felt like I knew my mom. She wasn't a stranger to me anymore. What I'd learned about her life and her death allowed me to finally let go and say good-bye.

Dear Mom,

Who would have thought the word "Mom" would sound so foreign? It's the first word a child utters and the only word to mean unconditional love. Writing to you is strange because not only have you been in heaven with the angels for twenty-six years, but I was so young when you died you have only been a mere image in my life.

Confident your gracious family would do right by your children, I'm sure you were rolling over in your grave the day Bill brought us back to New Hampshire after your funeral. I often imagined you in heaven watching over James and Jason and me, seeing how lonely we were. I wondered what you thought about how our lives changed after your death.

It has been said that when a person loses a loved one there are so many questions left unanswered. Growing up I had my own vision and perception of who you were and the fate you met. I was comfortable with the place in my head I found for all the horror you endured. I'm guessing it was a safety mechanism, my subconscious protecting me from the truth until I was able to handle the reality. It has taken me many years to actually allow myself to visualize the brutality of your death.

Normal is what you know, especially in today's society when there are varying degrees of normal. I never understood how bizarre my childhood was until I had children of my own and a chance to see what real normalcy is supposed to look like. Being a mother myself has made me look at you in a different way, instead of the fantasy I created.

For awhile, I had haunting questions surrounding not only your death but your life as well. In my journey to find those answers, I learned that the choices you made so many years ago have impacted the decisions I now make everyday. I lived believing that if I never allowed myself to take the easy way out, rely on a man for my every need, I would have the opportunity to watch my children grow – something I regret you never had the chance to do. If you are thinking I am angry, I'm not. In my journey to discover the truth, I found you. I no longer have questions and I feel I know you better now than I ever did. I am delighted to know we are similar in personality. Being told that I am a lot like you is to me the greatest compliment.

I no longer have any anger about my childhood. I feel at peace now. I believe there is a reason for everything. As tragic as growing up on the farm was at times, I learned so much about life and adversity and what it takes to survive in this cruel world. Life is hard and the greatest blessings are the ones right in front of us.

So thank you, Mom, for showing me the examples of what I want to be, as well as what I will never be. Learning about you has made me see that I don't need to spend my life running from the past. I am my own person, living with the consequences of my own choices, not in the shadows of yours. I like me! It's taken a long time for me to be able to say that, but it's in great part due to the tools you gave me. The love you bestowed on me in ten short years made me capable of passing that love on to my own children.

I miss you every day and need you more the older I get, but I know that you are always with me. I love you, Mom.

After I wrote my last letter and sealed it in an envelope, I felt like a huge weight had been lifted off of me. I compiled them all and placed them at the bottom of my jewelry box. The only other item in the hand-carved cherry wood box was the necklace my mother had worn the night of her murder—a solid gold pendant with the scales of justice embedded in it. It was the only thing of my mother's that I possessed and it gave me a sense of comfort. I look forward to the day I can bring myself to put it on. When that day comes, who knows how it will inspire me!

But for now the box is now a symbol of my past and the doubt I had that true love was attainable for someone like me. Having finally made peace with my past, I was now able to focus on my future. I had come to accept that wonderful things could happen to me, including love. I looked down at the ring I had placed on my left hand years ago during my darkest days of divorce and early single parenthood—a beautiful emerald ring with two small diamonds on either side of a gold band. It was a daily reminder of failed relationships and broken promises. I took the ring off, placed it in the jewelry box with the letters to my family and my mother's necklace, and closed the lid.

The jewelry box sits on my bureau and everyday I look at it and I am reminded of better choices I can make. Every time my kids walk out the front door, I say to them, "Make good choices."

I'm not an overly religious person, but I do believe that I experienced what I did for a reason and that my life has a bigger purpose. My favorite saying, the one that got me through this difficult journey, is the serenity prayer "God, grant me the serenity to accept the things I can not change, to change the things I can and the wisdom to know the difference." I realize this is used for people trying to overcome addictions, but its truth has helped me move toward the future rather than live in the past.

It's not so much where I have been but where I am going that counts. I have finally accepted my childhood and believe I'm in a good place now. I realize that life is a series of choices, not just "the way it is," as I'd always thought. Everything that happened to me along the way made me who I am today, and I'm pretty happy with me. What could have been a tragic tale of a sad, haunted life turned into a realization that I was as blessed as I was cursed! I always thought God had cursed me with a beautiful smile to hide all the pain. Now I realize that he blessed me with an indomitable spirit from which to survive.

Epilogue

What started as a mission to share a crazy story of survival ended with closure, a means to an end so to speak. In writing this book I have found peace. I no longer blame anyone for what became my life after my mother's death. Although I used to like the idea that my life on the turkey farm was my secret, now that I have shared my story with others I feel vulnerable to their judgment. At the same time I feel free from the bondage that has held me hostage for years.

Without feeling as though I am making any apologies for the content of this book, I want to express my thoughts. This memoir is in no way meant to hurt or speak badly about anyone. Unfortunately for me, my family is not the kind that I can sit down with and talk to about my feelings or how something they did affected me. I can't reminisce about the past and tell them how I felt then or even how I feel now. Through this book I have a voice and hopefully my family will respect and appreciate that it was my way of finding healing to my painful past.

For so long I have lived with wishing and wondering how things would have been had my mother made different choices in her life. Until now, I'd never realized how thinking that way prevented me from moving forward. My mom's choice to make a life with a man who exposed her to his dangerous world bore consequences that I will carry for a lifetime. In researching the time period in which my mother was raised, however, I have come to realize that the influences of that era had an enormous impact on the choices she made. I'm not blaming society or the changes happening in the world at that time but understanding it has helped me to understand her – it really was a different world back then. Unfortunately, my mom paid the ultimate price for her poor choices.

Just as we are affected by the choices made by our parents, there does come a time when we must take responsibility for our own lives and our own actions. I could have easily followed down a similar path to that of which I was raised, placing blame on everyone that hurt me, and there were many. Instead, I made an important choice, one that changed the course of my life back in the right direction. I choose not to allow my childhood, my past, to define me or to use it as an excuse for my failures, but to rise above it. We are only human and have moments of weakness – a zig when you should have zagged. Some people live in the midst of the consequence of their bad decision making while others are able to put it into their memory bank, learn from it and move forward. Fortunately, I was able to do that. I too have made some poor choices in my life and done things I'm not very proud of. But I learned to hold my head up high and look for the lesson. It's the lessons learned and the lessons taught that make life and every experience, good or bad, worth it.

That being said, I have been a clinical nurse on an Alzheimer's unit for over ten years. When I first went into nursing I thought I would follow in my mother's footsteps and fulfill her dream of being a pediatric nurse. Call it fate or destiny, but I ended up in geriatrics and I love it. Every day I help the helpless. I have often wondered where my deep sense of compassion came from, now I realize that it comes from what my mom taught me in my formative years before she died.

When a patient gets close to death, it doesn't upset me. I used to think that made me cold hearted. Instead, I feel a sense of peace, as I know they are going to a better place. That is not to say that when one of my favorites passes away I don't get a little tug at my heart but when I know their final breath is coming and I go in to say good-bye, I give them a kiss on the forehead and say, "Tell my mom I say hi."

When I wake up each day, I ask myself, "What difference can I make in someone's life today?" It gives me a reason to get up in the morning. Up until now it has been for my kids, my nursing and for this book. Now that my kids are grown and the book is done, my desire to help the elderly has moved beyond direct patient care. My hope is to bring awareness to the needs of the growing elderly population.

My daughter Katelyn, a high school junior, is on a hockey scholarship at a Prep school in New Hampton. My son Jaran will be attending the same school next year. Although their father (my ex-husband) is much more involved in their lives now, he continues to try and make my life a living hell using the kids and my past as his ammunition. Unfortunately, I have learned the hard way, as I usually do, that the Family Court system is disgustingly screwed up. In the end, it doesn't matter how good of a parent I am; it's all about how much money Tim has to pay a good lawyer (all the makings of a great sequel!)

While writing this book I had a third child, a boy. He is the consequence of a moment of weakness, a one-night stand. At first, I was very surprised and a bit disappointed. My other two were getting older and more independent, leaving some time for me. But even though he wasn't conceived under the most moral of circumstances, I realized that he was a blessing in disguise, God's way of giving me a second chance. Redemption for the baby I chose not to have years earlier during my darkest days. This "little man" is now five years old and going to kindergarten. He has brought my big kids and me so much joy. I have never once regretted having him. I have also found true love with Steve and for the first time feel like I have a real family.

James is married with two children and works very hard to make a nice life for himself and his family. Jason is engaged to a wonderful woman and, although I worry about all that he has suppressed regarding our childhood, he has a great support system to help him when he is ready to face it. Bill is still a constant in my life and I've come to accept always will be. He is my dad and I love him, despite everything. Always the entrepreneur, he has a thriving landscaping business, which is very much legitimate and free of any hidden agendas. He's still the abrasive SOB he was while I was growing up, and when I stop by his place of business and hear him yelling and cursing at his employees I shake my head a little, smile and think, *Yeah, been there, done that!*

One of the things I've always told myself is that, no matter how bad I have it, someone, somewhere has it worse. I guess it was "self-talk" like that, that empowered me to hope for better days and persevere through the darkness that surrounded me. I also like to believe it was my mom whispering encouragement in my ear when I felt defeated. Understanding that the cards I'd been dealt in life were partly a result of the consequences of choices made by my parents and guardians was half the battle. Knowledge is power and the truth does set you free. Once I'd learned the truth about my mom, her life and her death, and came to understand why my dad, my Auntie and Nana made some of the choices they did, I felt a rebirth of myself. This enabled me to come to a place of acceptance, forgiveness and healing.

If my story inspires even one person to get through whatever trial he or she is enduring, I will have accomplished what I set out to do. With the right attitude and some help from above, you can get through anything and everything. Like my Nana always said, "God never gives you more then you can handle." Remember, as horrible and devastating as today is, there's always hope for tomorrow!

www.ingramcontent.com/pod-product-compliance
Lightning Source LLC
LaVergne TN
LVHW061213060426
835507LV00016B/1914